12 MONTHS OF FUN!

THE LOBSTER KIDS' GUIDE TO EXPLORING MONTRÉAL

REVISED EDITION

BY JOHN SYMON

D1445644

Lobster
Press
Limited

Symon, John, 1958-
The Lobster Kids' Guide to Exploring Montréal: 12 Months of Fun!
Text copyright © 2000 by Lobster Press Limited
Illustrations copyright © 2000 by Lobster Press Limited

Published by
Lobster Press Limited
1250 René-Lévesque Blvd. West, Suite 2200
Montréal, Québec H3B 4W8
Tel. (514) 989-3121, Fax (514) 989-3168
www.lobsterpress.com

Publisher: Alison Fripp
Editor: Kathy Tompkins
Managing Editor: Bob Kirner
Production Manager: Allison Larin
Editorial Intern: Alison Fischer
Researcher: Lorraine Leduc
Cover and Illustrations: Christine Battuz
Icons: Christiane Beauregard
Layout and Design: Olivier Lasser

Canadian Cataloguing-in-Publication Data
Includes index.
ISBN 1-894222-09-1

1. Family recreation—Québec (Province)—Montréal Region—
Guidebooks. 2. Amusements—Québec (Province)—Montréal
Region—Guidebooks. 3. Montréal Region (Québec)—Guidebooks.
I. Battuz, Christine. II. Title. III. Title: Twelve Months of Fun!
IV. Lobster Kids' Guide to Exploring Montréal, 1998-99.

FC2947.33.S95 1998   917.14'28044   C98-900522-4
F1054.5.M83S95 1998

Printed and bound in Canada

To my mother, who always encouraged me to write; to my children, who became enthusiastic guinea pigs; and to my wife, who tolerated all of this and made good lunches.

It would have been impossible to write this book without tremendous support and encouragement from my family, friends, and business associates. I especially want to thank Jenny and Dan, Louis-Jacques, Danielle and Danny, Tara, Robyn, Sabine, Susan, mapman, Tom and Sharon, Ray and Joanne, Bicycle Bob, Ingrid and Dave, Ed and Kim, and Nancy and Adama. And thank you, Carlos, for asking the right question.

My gratitude goes to Alison Fripp, publisher of Lobster Press, for taking a chance on a first-time author; to Bob Kirner, editor of the first edition, for his ability to spot and correct inconsistencies and his unfaltering cheerfulness throughout the many drafts of the manuscript; to acting editor Kathy Tompkins, for her labour on this revised edition, including finding space for all the new sites; to editorial intern Alison Fischer for the countless hours of additional research and indexing; and to the rest of the gang at Lobster Press for their fine work. Finally, a special thank you to my research assistant, Lorraine Leduc, for countless hours on the telephone double-checking facts.

> *"Raising children is probably the most important job you will ever do in your life."*
> JACQUELINE ONASSIS

Table of Contents

Author's Introduction

T he Lobster Kids' Guide series began unoffi-
cially in 1993, when my first-born was old
enough to enjoy adventures around Montréal.
As my family multiplied and grew, we visited many
sites in and around the city, and I kept detailed notes
of our outings, paying particular attention to places
that held special allure for children. I shared this
information with others on the lookout for kid-
friendly attractions. Over the years my notes became
quite voluminous, and I approached Lobster Press
about publishing them as a guide for families. They
were keen on the idea and sent us back out to do even
more reconnaissance. *The Lobster Kids' Guide to
Exploring Montréal* was the result.

My thanks to the public and to the media for so
enthusiastically receiving the first edition of this
guide in 1998—it became a best-seller. This edition,
completely revised, has updated information for all of
the sites that appeared in the first book. Also, I've
added 20 new destinations—many of which were sug-
gested by readers.

The Lobster Kids' Guide to Exploring Montréal is
written for families with children ages 1 to 12 but you
don't have to be a kid to use it, just a kid at heart. Have
fun!

JOHN SYMON

A Word from the Publisher

L obster Press is proud to present the revised edition of our first book, *The Lobster Kids' Guide to Exploring Montréal.* We've included new scheduling, pricing and program information for each site and even managed to squeeze in 20 new ones.

Whether you're a tourist, teacher, or parent, if you're caring for children between the ages of 1 and 12, this book is ideal for you. It's a complete resource of things to do and see with kids in the Montréal area, both indoors and out, through all four seasons and for all budgets.

The sites in this guide were all updated (and in many cases revisited) in 1999-2000 before going to press. However, since prices and opening hours are liable to change and roads are sometimes under construction and some sites close their doors, please accept our apologies in advance for any inconveniences you may encounter.

Take a moment to read about the "Lobster Rating System." It tells you what John Symon and his children thought of each site. Next, familiarize yourself with our icons. We designed them to provide information at a glance and also to make you smile.

Street names and addresses for each site are given in French with the English translation in brackets. This is to facilitate "getting there," as Québec street names on signs and in city maps are in French. Also, all distances to the sites and activities were determined from downtown Montréal. We think it's a good meeting point for east, west, north and south.

We welcome your comments. We couldn't include everything that's available for children in Montréal, so if you feel that we've missed one of your family's favourite destinations, please contact us and we'll consider it for the next edition.

A last word: Please be careful when you and your children visit the sites in this guide. Neither Lobster Press nor John Symon can be held responsible for any accidents you or your family might incur.

Enjoy! And watch for the other six books in The Lobster Kids' City Explorers series: The Lobster Kids' Guides to Exploring Ottawa-Hull, Vancouver, Toronto, Calgary, Halifax and Québec City.

FROM THE GANG AT LOBSTER PRESS

The Lobster Rating System

W e thought it would be helpful if you knew what the Symon family thought about the sites in this book before you head off to visit them. John and his wife and three children rated every attraction and activity they visited for its:

☞ enjoyment level for children
☞ learning opportunities for children
☞ accessibility from downtown Montréal
☞ costs and value for money

A one-lobster rating: Good attraction.

A two-lobster rating: Very good attraction.

A three-lobster rating: Excellent attraction.

Not fitting some of the criteria, and subsequently not rated, are green spaces and various similar, nearby or other attractions.

Table of Icons

T hese facilities and/or activities are represented by the following icons:

Beach		Metro station	
Bicycling		Parking	
Birthday parties		Picnic tables	
Bus stop		Playground	
Coat check		Restaurant/ snack bar	
Cross-country skiing		Skating	
Downhill skiing		Snowshoeing	
First aid		Swimming	
Heated chalet		Telephone	
Hiking		Tobogganing	
Ice cream stand		Toilets	
In-line skating		Wheelchair/stroller accessible	
Information centre		Wildlife watching	

Getting Ready

Once you've planned an activity for the day, why not take a few minutes and prepare for it. Nothing will ruin an outing faster than forgetting something important at home. These helpful suggestions will ensure your next outing is pleasant for everyone.

☞ Call ahead and verify the site's opening hours and prices.

☞ If you're travelling a considerable distance, pack healthy snacks for everyone.

☞ Remember to bring along liquids.

☞ Pack a road map and a first-aid kit, and be sure that anyone who is taking medication has it with them.

☞ Does anyone get car sick? Bring the Gravol™.

☞ Playing "I Spy," having singsongs and listening to your kids' favourite cassettes while on the road will make the drive more pleasant and delay the inevitable "Are we there yet?"

☞ You already know about packing diapers, wipes and spare clothes. But remember to pack a small toy or two for the baby to play with.

☞ Coloured pencils and scratch pads keep little hands busy on a long drive and while waiting for a restaurant meal.

☞ If you're visiting a park, bring along a Frisbee™, a Hacky Sack™ or a soccer ball.

☞ After a long car ride, take the children to a park before heading to a museum or similar site.

☞ Pack insect repellent, sunscreen, swimsuits, towels and hats if it's summer and you're going to an outdoor site.

☞ Bring extra hats, gloves, scarves, boots and warm coats for outdoor winter activities. Dress in layers, wearing a polycotton or other moisture-releasing fabric next to your body. A dab of Vaseline™ applied to cheeks and noses reduces the risk of frostbite—so can running to the nearest canteen for hot chocolate!

☞ This book uses the metric system where distance is measured in kilometres, height in centimetres, weight in kilograms and area in hectares. Also, temperature is measured in centigrade. For those unfamiliar with these units:

➤ One kilometre is just over a half mile (0.62 miles).

➤ The minimum height requirement for certain midway rides and waterslides is 122 centimetres (4 feet).

➤ One kilogram is equivalent to a little more than two pounds (2.2 pounds).

➤ One hectare is approximately the same area as two and a half acres (2.47 acres).

➤ Water freezes at 0°C (32°F). When the temperature's 25°C (77°F) it's shorts and T-shirt weather.

Bon voyage!

Getting Around with Young Children

S ome of the sites in this guide are located on expansive grounds and are only accessible on foot. This may be problematic for parents with children in strollers, especially if the walk is over rough terrain. In this guide, sites indicated as being wheelchair accessible are suitable for strollers as well.

TRANSPORTING BABIES

Instead of using a stroller, you might consider carrying your child in a Snugli™. When babies grow out of their Snuglies™ and can hold their heads up properly, they're old enough to be transported in child carrier backpacks. Backpacks are ideal for all types of terrain.

BICYCLING WITH CHILDREN

Today, more and more parents want to include their children on long-distance bicycle rides. If your kids are too young to ride on their own, you can carry them in children's bike seats or in a trailer or trail-a-bike. Used alone or in combination, these accessories provide safe and worry-free bicycling for the entire family. Remember to fit your children with approved bicycle helmets.

CROSS-COUNTRY SKIING WITH SMALL CHILDREN

Even if children lack the technique and stamina to cross-country ski, families can still enjoy a day on the trails using one of two devices for carrying them. A carrier backpack is ideal as long as the adult who is wearing it is a strong skier and avoids steep hills. You can also use a ski trailer. Hiking and bicycle shops carry a variety of makes, but keep your eyes open for quality models such as Scandinavia's Ski-pjulken. Though remember, while the skiers in your party are working up a sweat, any youngster who's in a ski trailer is lying in the cold.

If carrying and hauling your children is wearing you down, maybe it's time to look into cross-country skiing lessons for them. Angrignon Park in Montréal, the Viking Ski Club in the Laurentians, and the YMCA offer courses for children ages three and up.

CHAPTER 1

LOCAL ATTRACTIONS

Introduction

There's no shortage of attractions in and around Montréal that offer fun-filled activities for families. Whichever direction you head in, it will be a pathway to discovery and excitement for your children.

A short car ride east (a bit longer by the metro) brings you to three premier biological exhibits within minutes of each other. Indulge your youngsters' passion for plants at the Montréal Botanical Garden. There's always a fascinating exhibit that's geared to kids. The Insectarium has hands-on displays and live exhibits that will satisfy any kid's curiosity about insects. How about a stroll through a tropical forest? The Biodome is where you'll find this and other living ecosystems.

Read on to find out about these local attractions in greater detail. This chapter also includes: hot licks and cool blues at the Montréal International Jazz Festival, ice-skating at a downtown skyscraper; riding a cable car up the world's tallest leaning tower; stargazing at the planetarium; exploring an ancient cavern and more.

Chill Out
AT THE BIODOME

4777 AV. PIERRE-DE COUBERTIN (PIERRE DE COUBERTIN AVE.)
MONTRÉAL
(514) 868-3000 OR 872-2237 EXT. 622
WWW.VILLE.MONTREAL.QC.CA/BIODOME

Visiting the Biodome is the next best thing to being in a tropical jungle. Located at the Olympic Park, this research and education centre has living recreations of the Amazon rainforest, the Laurentian woods, the Gulf of St. Lawrence estuary and the Arctic and Antarctic polar worlds that are complete with native plants and animals. Each ecosystem is housed in a large climate-controlled space and only glass walls and elevated walkways separate you from the animals.

You can feel the humidity on your walk through the Amazon region, which features dozens of tropical birds that are free and flying

☞ **SEASONS AND TIMES**
➤ Year-round: Daily, 9 am–6 pm (until 8 pm in the summer).

☞ **COST**
➤ Adults $9.50, seniors and students $7, children (6 to 17) $4.75, under 6 free.

☞ **GETTING THERE**
➤ By car, take Sherbrooke St. east to Viau St. Go south to Pierre de Coubertin Ave. and turn west. Pay parking on site. Some free parking on nearby streets. About 20 minutes from downtown.
➤ By public transit, take the metro (green line) to the Viau station. You'll have a five-minute walk. A free shuttle service links the Biodome, Botanical Garden, Insectarium, Olympic Park and the Viau metro station.
➤ By bicycle, follow car directions.

☞ **NEARBY**
➤ Botanical Garden, Insectarium and Olympic Park.

☞ **COMMENT**
➤ Plan a 1-hour visit.

overhead. Children will thrill to the antics of the body surfing penguins at the Antarctic exhibit. Or, check out the enormous fish at the Gulf of St. Lawrence marine display, or the cutaway beaver lodge at the Laurentian exhibit. After your tour, head to the Naturalia Discovery Room in the basement where hands-on activities such as comparing skeletons let you learn more about animals and their environment.

The Biodome offers tours to groups and has a free outreach program for schools. Call 868-3056.

Swinging into Summer
THE MONTRÉAL INTERNATIONAL JAZZ FESTIVAL

175 RUE STE-CATHERINE O. (ST. CATHERINE ST. W.)
AND OTHER DOWNTOWN LOCATIONS
(514) 523-3378 (OFFICE), (514) 871-1881
(INFORMATION AND TICKETS), 1-888-515-0515
WWW.MONTREALJAZZFEST.COM

☞ **SEASONS AND TIMES**
➤ Late June and early July. Activities usually start in the early afternoon.

☞ **COST**
➤ Activities for families are free.

☞ **GETTING THERE**
➤ By public transit, take the metro (green line) to the Place des Arts station.

For many Mont-réalers, the Jazz Fest signals the beginning of summer. In late June and early July music's in the air as performers and aficionados from around the world fill the downtown streets, nightclubs and cafés. Many of the streets are closed to traffic to make room for the toe-tapping crowds.

Although primarily a venue for adults, the Jazz Fest has attractions for families, too. The Petite École du Jazz at Place des Arts, a series of afternoon concerts conducted by comedian Jacques L'Heureux, introduces children to the basics of jazz music and invites them to participate by singing and clapping along.

The outdoor Music Park, located next to Place des Arts on St. Catherine, is a playground with music as its theme. Kids can play on an assortment of inflatable toys shaped like musical instruments or express their musical side by stepping on the keys of the giant keyboard to make it play. Face painting at the Music Park is so popular that reservations are recommended. By grabbing a bite at the nearby food court you won't have to miss a single beat of the fun. Families can also take in jugglers, acrobats, clowns and other entertainers who perform on the streets around the festival.

Making a Splash at THE AQUADOME

1411 RUE LAPIERRE (LAPIERRE ST.)
LASALLE
(514) 367-6460

T his indoor aquatic fitness centre is bound to be a hit with anybody who enjoys swimming, splashing around, or hanging out beside the pool. The Aquadome features three pools including a shallow one for younger children. It's equipped with waterslides and colourful foam flotation aids—the large ones shaped like fish are kids' favourites. Stretch out on a comfy chaise longue and watch your kids carry on.

There are regularly scheduled times when families can go swimming and lessons are offered to children as young as six months. The centre also has a wide range of aquatic sports available to all ages.

You can make arrangements to hold a child's birthday party here. Packages that include indoor rock climbing at CEGEP

☞ **SEASONS AND TIMES**
➤Year-round: Families, Mon—Fri, 5:30 pm—7 pm, (until 9 pm on Fri); Splash pool, Mon, Wed, Thu, Fri, 9 am—3:55 pm. For a complete schedule of activities, call 367-6460.

☞ **COST**
➤ Non-residents: Adults $3, seniors and children (4 to 16) $2, under 4 free. Discount for LaSalle residents.

☞ **GETTING THERE**
➤ By car, take Hwy. 15 S. to de la Vérendrye Blvd. Exit and go west to Lapierre St., then turn north. The Aquadome is beside CEGEP André Laurandeau. Free parking on site. You must register your car in the guest book. About 20 minutes from downtown.
➤ By public transit, take the metro (green line) to the Angrignon station and transfer to the 113 bus. It's a short ride.

André Laurandeau are available. Ask the Aquadome's management for details.

☞ **SIMILAR ATTRACTIONS**

➤ These indoor swimming centres have programs and facilities
for kids and most have splash pools for toddlers.
There's a complete listing of Montréal area municipal pools on
page 85.

CEPSUM at the Université de Montréal
2100 boul. Édouard-Montpetit (Édouard Montpetit Blvd.)
Montréal (514) 343-6150

Little Burgundy Sport Centre
1825 rue Notre-Dame (Notre Dame St.)
Montréal (514) 932-0800

Olympic Park Sports Centre
3200 rue Viau (Viau St.)
Montréal (514) 252-4622
(six pools, waterslides)

Rivière-des-Prairies pool
12515 boul. Rodolphe-Forget (Rodolphe Forget Blvd.)
Montréal (514) 872-9322
(bring your own flotation devices)

Pointe Claire YMCA
230 boul. Brunswick (Brunswick Blvd.)
Pointe-Claire (514) 630-9622
(tarzan swings and waterslides)

Stopping to Smell the Flowers at THE MONTRÉAL BOTANICAL GARDEN

4101 RUE SHERBROOKE E. (SHERBROOKE ST. E.)
MONTRÉAL
(514) 872-1400 OR 872-2237 EXT. 621
WWW.VILLE.MONTREAL.QC.CA/JARDIN

☞ **SEASONS AND TIMES**
→ Year-round: Daily, 9 am–5 pm (until 7 pm in summer).

☞ **COST**
→ Summer: May–Oct, adults $9.50, seniors $7, children(6 to 17) $4.75, under 5 free.
Winter: Nov–Apr, adults $6.75, seniors $5.25, children(6 to 17) $3.50, under 5 free.

☞ **GETTING THERE**
→ By car, take Sherbrooke St. east to Pie IX Blvd. Pay parking on site. About 20 minutes from downtown.
→ By public transit, take the metro (green line) to the Pie-IX station and follow the signs or go to the Viau station and catch the free shuttle linking the Botanical Garden with the Insectarium, the Biodome and the Olympic Park.
→ By bicycle, follow car directions.

Something's always in bloom at the Botanical Garden. The garden boasts the second largest plant collection in the world (over 26,000 varieties) in ten greenhouses and numerous outdoor settings.

In the greenhouses you'll find all kinds of exotic species such as banana trees, orchids, prickly desert cacti and much more. Showcasing the outdoor sites are the Chinese Garden, with its pagodas and lanterns, and the elegant Japanese Garden, where you'll find a delightful collection of bonsai trees in the summer. Children will love exploring the tree house which doubles as a tree learning centre. Bring your cameras and binoculars. The garden features many beautiful backdrops for photos and is home to several bird species.

> ☞ **NEARBY**
> ➤ Olympic Park, Biodome and Insectarium.
>
> ☞ **COMMENT**
> ➤ Plan a half-day visit. There's a free shuttle that circles the grounds.

The Botanical Garden has seasonal displays on pumpkin carving, Chinese lanterns, and vegetable gardening. It also sponsors a young gardeners' club, giving children ages 11 to 15 the chance to grow their own vegetables. Charges apply. Many programs are offered to school groups. Call 872-1446 for more information. There's a free tour for teachers, call 872-7959.

Catch a Falling Star at THE MONTRÉAL PLANETARIUM

1000 RUE ST-JACQUES (ST. JACQUES ST.)
MONTRÉAL
(514) 872-4530 OR 872-2237 EXT. 623
WWW.PLANETARIUM.MONTREAL.QC.CA

S itting in the Planetarium is like being in a movie theatre. But instead of watching the action unfold on a screen in front of them, audiences have to look up to the large vaulted roof. That's where the planetarium plays its celestial

☞ **SEASONS AND TIMES**
→Year-round: Tue—Sun.
Call 872-4530 for information about upcoming features and their times.

☞ **COST**
→ Adults $6, seniors and students $4.50, children (6 to 17) $3, under 6 free.

☞ **GETTING THERE**
→ By car, turn south on Peel St. from René-Lévesque Blvd. and follow the signs to the Planetarium. Free parking on site. Minutes from downtown.
→ By public transit, take the metro (orange line) to the Bonaventure station. It's a five-minute walk from there.
→ By bicycle, use the car directions.

☞ **COMMENT**
→ Late arrivals are not admitted. Alternating French and English presentations.

show. A special projector makes it possible to view the moon, planets and stars and changes their positions, demonstrating how the night sky appears at any given place or time on Earth.

Shows with other themes, including meteorites, time measurement, celestial collisions and black holes, are presented. Some are followed by workshops. School groups may attend an introductory lecture about the planetarium and free outreach programs are available. Call 868-3056.

Exploring THE BIOSPHERE

160 RUE TOUR-DE-L'ÎSLE (TOUR DE L'ÎSLE RD.)
ÎLE STE-HÉLÈNE (ST. HELEN'S ISLAND)
MONTRÉAL
(514) 283-5000
HTTP://BIOSPHERE.EC.GC.CA

Not to be confused with the Biodome, the Biosphere, located in the geodesic dome that housed the American pavilion during Expo '67, is an interactive museum and ecowatch observation centre devoted to the St. Lawrence River and Great Lakes ecosystems.

The centre's movies, user-friendly computers, scale models, multimedia shows and workshops all foster public awareness of the importance of clean water. Most of the displays are geared to children over six. Younger children will be happy pushing buttons and visiting the goldfish pond or the discovery area on the main floor. Animators are present daily between 10 am

☞ **SEASONS AND TIMES**
➤ Winter: Oct—May, Tue—Sat,
10 am—5 pm.
Summer: June—Sept, daily,
10 am—6 pm.

☞ **COST**
➤ Adults $6.50, seniors and students $5, children (6 to 17) $4, under 6 free, families $16.

☞ **GETTING THERE**
➤ By car, take the Jacques Cartier Bridge south and follow the signs for La Ronde. Once on Île Ste-Hélène, look for the posted signs to the Biosphere. Free parking in lot P8. About 20 minutes from downtown.
➤ By public transit, take the metro (yellow line) to the Île Ste-Hélène station. It's a five-minute walk from there.
➤ By bicycle, follow the Lachine Canal from the Old Port, but turn south towards Cité du Havre. Access the Concorde bridge and go over the river and turn east at the first exit and continue on to the Biosphere.

☞ **NEARBY**
➤ Stewart Museum, Parc-des-Îles.

☞ **COMMENT**
➤ Plan a 1-hour visit. Extra fees may apply to some exhibits, including the children's workshop.

and 5 pm in the summer and children can read books, dig in a sandbox and learn how to draw underwater.

Tours are offered to school groups with a reservation (496-8282). For information on the Biosphere's educational workshops, call 496-8300.

Ice-skating at the Atrium
LE 1000 DE LA GAUCHETIÈRE

1000 RUE DE LA GAUCHETIÈRE O. (DE LA GAUCHETIÈRE ST. W.)
MONTRÉAL
(514) 395-0555
WWW.LE**1000**.COM

☞ **SEASONS AND TIMES**
➤ Year-round: Public skating, Sun–Thu, 11:30 am–9 pm; Fri–Sat, 11:30 am–7 pm. DJ on ice (16 and over only) Fri–Sat, 7 pm–midnight.

☞ **COST**
➤ Adults $5, seniors and children (under 16) $3. Group rates available. Rentals: Skates $4, children's helmets $1.50, lockers $1.

If you're looking for a cool way to beat the heat this summer, take the family skating at the Atrium. This indoor rink, located in a downtown skyscraper, is open year-round and because it's built in an atrium, there's an abundance of sunlight on clear days.

Mornings are reserved for groups, but public skating dominates the schedule from just before noon onward. Equipment such as skates, helmets and walkers for first-time skaters can be rented. The Atrium also has special events and organized activities for children including birthday parties. For more information, call 395-4806.

The off-ice atmosphere is just as pleasant. There is a food court that's mainly smoke-free and with nearly a dozen food concessions to choose from, even the most finicky eater is sure to be satisfied.

☞ **GETTING THERE**
→ By car, take de la Cathédrale south from René Lévesque Blvd. Indoor pay parking on site, pay parking lots nearby.
→ By public transit, take the metro (orange line) to the Bonaventure station and follow the posted signs. The Atrium is under the same roof as the South Shore bus terminus and is a short stroll from the commuter trains at Windsor and Central stations.
→ By bicycle, follow the car directions. Bicycle parking is available.

☞ **NEARBY**
→ Montréal Stock Exchange, Peregrine Falcon Information Centre, Montréal Planetarium.

Visiting the Crèche Exposition at ST. JOSEPH'S ORATORY

3800 Ch. Queen Mary (Queen Mary Rd.)
Montréal
(514) 733-8211

St. Joseph's Oratory, on Mount Royal's northwestern slope, is a famous Montréal landmark attracting nearly two million visitors

☞ **SEASONS AND TIMES**
➤ Crèches Exposition: Mid-Nov—
mid-Feb, daily, 10 am—5 pm.
Basilica and Museum of Brother
André: Year-round, daily, 7 am—
5:30 pm.
Exhibits and Museum of the Holy
Family: Year-round, daily, 10 am—
5 pm.
Organ concerts: Year-round, Sun,
3:30 pm.
Carillon: Wed—Fri, 12 pm and
3 pm; weekends, noon and 2:30 pm.

☞ **COST**
➤ Free (donations are accepted).

☞ **GETTING THERE**
➤ By car, take Côte-des-Neiges Rd.
north to Queen Mary Rd. and turn
west. Free parking on site. A shuttle
operates from the parking lot to the
Oratory. About 10 minutes from
downtown.
➤ By public transit, take STCUM
buses 51 or 166. The Côte-des-
Neiges metro station is about
a 10-minute walk away.

☞ **NEARBY**
➤ Mount Royal Park.

☞ **COMMENT**
➤ Plan a 1-hour visit. Not wheelchair
accessible. It can get very hot
at the exposition and there is no coat
check.

each year. The Oratory features many splendid exhibits, such as the Basilica; the tomb of Brother André, who founded the Oratory; the Museum of the Holy Family; art collections and other treasures; however, they may not hold the attention of younger children very long.

What kids will like best is attending the exposition of crèches (Nativity scenes) on display between November and February. The Oratory's collection comprises nearly 300 scenes from about 100 countries and includes figurines that are small enough to hold in your hands as well as life-size recreations. Many art styles and mediums are represented and show an incredible variation in interpreting one event. The exposition is delightful and every child will relate to the scene of a baby who's surrounded by animals.

Buzzing around
THE INSECTARIUM

4581 RUE SHERBROOKE E. (SHERBROOKE ST. E.)
MONTRÉAL
(514) 872-1400
WWW.VILLE.MONTREAL.QC.CA/INSECTARIUM

E ven if you think bugs are creepy, at least you'll come away from the Insectarium appreciating them. You may even start to like them. On display in this museum devoted to insects are living and preserved specimens, and a wealth of information on insect ecology and their behaviour too. Among the exhibits kids like best are the live tarantulas and scorpions, and the collection of dazzling butterflies from around the world. Nearby maps will show them the route monarch butterflies follow during their migration to Mexico. There is a working bee hive to investigate and exhibits that demonstrate the important roles insects play to keep the Earth healthy. Kids can even design their own insect using a computer.

In the summer you can visit the Butterfly Tent outdoors, which is the home of butterfly

☞ **SEASONS AND TIMES**
➤ Winter: Sept—mid-June, daily, 10 am—5 pm.
Summer: Mid-June—Sept, daily, 10 am—7 pm.

☞ **COST**
➤ Adults $9.50, seniors and children (6 to 17) $7, under 6 $4.75.

☞ **GETTING THERE**
➤ By car, take Sherbrooke St. east until Pie IX Blvd. Pay parking on site ($5). About 20 minutes from downtown.
➤ By public transit, take the metro (green line) to the Pie-IX or Viau stations. A free shuttle links the Biodome, Botanical Garden, Insectarium, Olympic Stadium and the Viau metro station.
➤ By bicycle, follow the car directions.

☞ **NEARBY**
→ Olympic Park, Biodome, Botanical Garden.

☞ **COMMENT**
→ Plan a 2-hour visit.

☞ **SIMILAR ATTRACTION**
→ **Lyman Entomological Museum, Centennial Building,** Macdonald Agricultural College, Ste. Anne de Bellevue (514) 398-7914. This research institute has a large collection of specimens for viewing by groups as young as kindergarten age. Appointment required.

species that are native to Québec. Usually, they're flitting between flowers and sipping nectar, though if you remain still long enough one might land on you.

The Insectarium has changing exhibits and demonstrations throughout the year dealing with bees and honey, the history of insect collecting, butterflies, recipes using bugs and other topics.

Other Local Attractions

The St. Léonard Cavern

5200 BOUL. LAVOISIER (LAVOISIER BLVD.)
ST. LÉONARD
(514) 252-3323 (INFORMATION), (514) 252-3006
OR 1-800-338-6636 (RESERVATION)
WWW.SPELEO.QC.CA

I f exploring cold, wet, dark places sounds like fun, consider a trip to the St. Léonard Cavern, a 40-metre-long cave formed about 15,000 years ago. Children as young as six are welcome to go on the 90-minute guided tours as long as they're accompanied by an adult. The ceiling is more than two metres high throughout most of the cave although it drops to about a metre toward the end, so be prepared to do some crawling.

Dress in old, warm clothing as the temperature underground is a constant 5°C. Bring a change of clothes (don't forget socks!) and a big plastic bag for your dirty clothes. Rubber boots and wool socks are the recommended footwear as there's always water in the cave. You will be provided with a miner's helmet equipped with a lamp. Up to 16 people can be accommodated at a time and reservations are necessary.

☞ Early June—late Aug, Tue—Sun, by reservation only.

☞ $3 for St. Léonard residents, $6.50 for non-residents, by cheque two weeks in advance payable to the Québec Speleological Society.

☞ Take Hwy. 40 east to Exit 76 then go north on Viau Blvd. to Lavoisier Blvd. About 15 minutes from downtown.

☞ Take the metro (green line) to the Viau station then transfer to STCUM bus 132 and ride it to Lavoisier Blvd. From there, walk east for two blocks to the cave site.

The Olympic Park

4141 AV. PIERRE-DE COUBERTIN (PIERRE DE COUBERTIN AVE.)
MONTRÉAL
(514) 252-8687
WWW.RIO.GOUV.QC.CA

Even if heights make you queasy, you might still enjoy the cable car ride at the Montréal Tower, the world's tallest leaning tower. In under two minutes, it carries you to the Olympic Park Observatory where there's a panoramic view of Montréal and its surroundings. If it's a clear day, you will be able to see as far as 80 kilometres. One level down there's a hall that presents exhibitions and special events.

For an extra fee, you can attend a multimedia show about Montreal's history and culture in the theatre at the base of the tower. The Olympic Park also houses the Olympic Stadium, home of the Montréal Expos baseball club, and the Olympic Park Sports Centre, which has six swimming pools including a wading pool with slides and games for toddlers. There is public swimming and swimming instruction available for all ages as well as courses in scuba diving, lifesaving and diving. Fitness programs and a summer day camp are offered to youths.

☞ For observatory, cable car and stadium tour schedules, call 252-8687. For sports centre schedule, call 252-4622.

☞ Observatory (including exhibit centre): Adults $9, children $5.50.
Olympic Stadium tours: Adults $5.50, children (17 and under) $4.25.
Multimedia show: Adults $8, children (17 and under) $5.50.
Sports Centre: Subject to registration.

☞ Take Sherbrooke St. east to Viau St. and turn south, then south again on Pierre de Coubertin Ave. Pay parking on site. Some free parking on nearby streets. About 20 minutes from downtown.

☞ Take the metro (green line) to the Viau station. There's a five-minute walk.

The St. Lambert Locks

NEAR THE VICTORIA BRIDGE
(450) 672-4110

The facilities at the St. Lambert Locks offer families the best spot for watching ships slip through the St. Lawrence Seaway and learning about its history. Inside the observation tower, which is open to the public although not accessible to wheelchairs, there's a video that explains the workings of the locks and photos to look at of the Seaway that have bilingual captions.

Children will delight in seeing how the locks work to lift or lower a ship several metres in just a few minutes. Then, when the gates swing open, watch the surprise on their faces as the Victoria Bridge is raised high into the air to let the vessel move on.

Most of the ships that use the Seaway are lakers, which fit easily inside the locks. Ocean-going vessels, however, are much larger and have but a few feet of clearance on either side of their hulls. Standing on the shore, you could reach out and touch one but why not settle for hailing a sailor instead.

☞ Year-round, or as long as the Seaway is ice-free.

☞ Free.

☞ The locks are best accessed from Hwy. 132 S. from Longueuil. Take the Jacques Cartier Bridge to Hwy. 132 S. and continue until Exit 3E (Sir Wilfrid Laurier Blvd.)—it's just after the Victoria Bridge. The road makes a "U" and turns left. There are posted signs. Free parking on site. About 25 minutes from downtown.

☞ Take South Shore Transit Authority buses 13 or 15.

SIMILAR ATTRACTIONS
☞ Hand-operated locks can be seen on the Chambly Canal next to Fort Chambly (page 202) and at Ste. Anne de Bellevue.

CHAPTER 2

OLD MONTRÉAL
&
THE OLD PORT

Introduction

1-800-971-PORT
WWW.OLDPORTOFMONTREAL.COM

Something exciting is always happening in Old Montréal. Its narrow, cobblestone streets, old architecture and trendy boutiques give it a European charm that's popular with tourists and Montréalers alike.

Regardless of the season, you can hire a calèche and tour the old city. Keep your eyes peeled for Notre Dame Basilica, at one time North America's largest church. Look for Champ de Mars behind City Hall where soldiers once performed military manoeuvres. You can still see parts of the wall that once protected the old city.

In the summer, stroll through Place Jacques Cartier and see street performers and artists plying their trade. Or, sit back on a restaurant terrasse and simply soak up the atmosphere. Perhaps you'd prefer to rent a quadracycle or in-line skates at the Old Port and tour the Promenade. Discover ice-skating on the Bonsecours Basin. Visit three popular museums with displays about Montréal's history, archaeology and banking. Enjoy sleigh rides, or visit a farmer's market. You'll be amazed at how many family attractions are offered in this historic section of Montréal.

Time Travel at the MONTRÉAL MUSEUM OF HISTORY

335 PLACE D'YOUVILLE
OLD MONTRÉAL
(514) 872-3207
WWW.VILLE.MONTREAL.QC.CA/CHM/CHM.HTM

Ninety minutes is all it will take your family to stroll through 350 years of Montréal's history. This museum, located in a former fire station, has 12 exhibits that trace the city's evolution from a tiny, fortified French outpost in 1642 to today's modern metropolis. You'll find unexpected displays such as trash cans as well as a tram car and a full-scale front of a typical Montréal duplex, complete with a wrought iron staircase that kids love to climb. There are also interactive videos and games, slide shows, buttons you can press, things to smell and life-size exhibits you can walk through. Although the

☞ **SEASONS AND TIMES**
➤ Winter: Feb—Nov, Tue—Sun,
10 am—5 pm.
Summer: May—Labour Day, daily,
10 am—5 pm.

☞ **COST**
➤ Adults $4.50, students and children $3, under 6 free.

☞ **GETTING THERE**
➤ By car, take René Lévesque Blvd. to Beaver Hall Hill and turn south (it becomes McGill St.). Turn east onto Place d'Youville. Pay and metered parking. Minutes from downtown.
➤ By public transit, take the metro (orange line) to the Square-Victoria station, exit via McGill St. and walk south.

☞ **NEARBY**
➤ Pointe à Callière Museum, Bank of Montréal Museum, Old Port.

☞ **COMMENT**
➤ At press time there were tentative plans to close the museum for renovations between July and December 2000. Call before you visit.

museum has few facilities, you'll find telephones, picnic tables and restaurants nearby.

Keeping Time
THE CLOCK TOWER

CLOCK TOWER PIER
OLD MONTRÉAL
(514) 496-PORT

☞ **SEASONS AND TIMES**
➤ May—Sept. Hours vary, call to confirm.

☞ **COST**
➤ Free. Donations accepted.

☞ **GETTING THERE**
➤ By car, take Réne Lévesque Blvd. to Berri St. and turn south. Continue along Berri until de la Commune St. and turn west. Pay and metered parking. Minutes from downtown.
➤ By public transit, take the metro (orange line) to the Champ-de-Mars station. Walk south on Gosford St. to Notre Dame St. and turn east to Berri St. Walk south on Berri to de la Commune St. and turn west. Walk south to the Clock Tower.

☞ **COMMENT**
➤ Children's Playground is open year-round.

Built in 1922 and still ticking, the Clock Tower has become a symbol of Montréal's old port. Originally erected to commemorate the men of the Merchant Fleet who died in the First World War, the Clock Tower underwent restoration in 1984 and now houses an observatory and an interpretation centre.

Step inside and see the displays highlighting Montréal's history. You'll learn interesting details about the tower, too—did you know it once served as a lighthouse? That done, hike up 192 stairs for a spectacular view of the cityscape and river.

Kids will love peering into the clock's mechanisms. If your youngsters still have energy after climbing the tower, head to the nearby Children's Playground that has slides, a suspension bridge, spring games and swings.

Digging for Facts at the POINTE À CALLIÈRE MUSEUM OF ARCHAEOLOGY AND HISTORY

350 PLACE ROYALE
OLD MONTRÉAL
(514) 872-9150
WWW.MUSEE-POINT-A-CALLIERE.QC.CA

T hanks to modern electronics, you can talk to ghosts at Pointe à Callière. The virtual figures are just one of many interactive exhibits the archaeological and historical museum uses to help visitors appreciate the artifacts it has on display that were once buried at this site.

Go on an interactive guided tour or guide yourself, beginning with a multi-media show about

☞ **SEASONS AND TIMES**
➛ Winter: Sept—June, Tue—Sat, 10 am—5 pm.
Summer: June—Sept, Mon—Fri, 11 am—6 pm; weekends, 10 am—6 pm.

☞ **COST**
➛ Adults $8.50, seniors $6, students $5.50, children (6 to 12) $2, under 6 free, families $17.

☞ **GETTING THERE**

➤ By car, take René Lévesque Blvd. to Beaver Hall Hill and turn south (it becomes McGill St.). Turn east onto Place d'Youville. Pay and metered parking.

➤ By public transit, take the metro (orange line) to the Place-d'Armes station and walk south on St. François Xavier St.

☞ **NEARBY**

➤ Montréal History Museum, Old Port, Lachine Canal.

☞ **COMMENT**

➤ Plan a 90-minute visit, and 15 minutes more for the pump house. An outdoor 18th century market staffed by museum volunteers in period costume takes place at Place Royale in late August.

Montréal's history. Then, move downstairs to the archaeological digs. The museum is built over the spot where Montréal was founded and you can view vestiges of Montréal's first Catholic cemetery, private houses and warehouses.

Across the street from the museum is the old sewer pumping station. Kids will enjoy dropping coloured balls into the model showing water drainage and pushing the "on" button to replicate the sound of the pumps.

The museum has workshops and tours for school groups. Activities include trying on period clothing, playing with toys that children of the early settlers of New France would have enjoyed and touching some of the museum's artifacts. Many of the items were uncovered in the archaeologists' treasure trove—an old outhouse pit. Outreach kits are available (872-9127) and tours for teachers can be arranged (872-9132).

Outdoor Skating on BONSECOURS BASIN

(FACING BONSECOURS MARKET)
350 RUE ST-PAUL E. (ST. PAUL ST. E.)
OLD MONTRÉAL
(514) 496-7678 OR 1-800-971-7678
WWW.OLDPORTOFMONTREAL.COM

The Bonsecours Basin is one of Montréal's most popular outdoor skating rinks. From its large circular surface, skaters have a marvellous view of Old Montréal's waterfront and the downtown skyline. The ice is artificial and refrigerated, so don't worry about mild snaps, and a Zamboni keeps it clean and smooth. There's no hockey playing here, just skating to the rhythm of the accompanying music. When you need a breather, wander over to the heated chalet and store your gear in a locker. Then, go exploring.

During the holiday season there's an elaborate nativity scene featuring actors and live animals. Watch a snowmobile demonstration, take a dog sled or sleigh ride, admire the ice sculptures or take your kids to the

☞ **SEASONS AND TIMES**
➤ Dec—Mar: Daily, 10 am—10 pm (weather permitting).

☞ **COST**
➤ $2, children under 6 free, season pass $10, family season pass $25. Skate rental $6 (includes admission). Free lockers, but bring a lock.

☞ **GETTING THERE**
➤ By car, take Beaver Hall Hill (it becomes McGill St.) south to de la Commune St. and then go east for a few blocks. Pay parking nearby. Minutes from downtown.
➤ By public transit, take the metro (orange line) to the Champ-de-Mars station and walk south on Gosford St.

☞ **NEARBY**
➤ IMAX™, Pointe à Callière Museum.

☞ **COMMENT**
➤ Plan a 2-hour visit. Strollers, but not sleds, are permitted on the ice.

☞ **SIMILAR ATTRACTIONS**

→ Beaver Lake
Mount Royal Park
Day and night skating. Sleigh rides. Heated chalet.
(514) 844-4928

→ Lafontaine Park
Sherbrooke St. and Parc Lafontaine Ave.
Day and night skating. Shelters.
Sherbrooke Metro

→ Olympic Basin
Parc des Îles, Île Notre Dame
One-kilometre long rink.
Île-Ste-Hélène Metro
(514) 872-6093

→ The Ice Palace
ch. Lake Echo and rte. 117, Prévost
One of the world's largest outdoor rinks.
(450) 224-8540

inflatable open-air playground at the Sun Life Village on Bonsecours Island. You can buy a Christmas tree or drop off donations for a food bank.

It gets windy beside the water, so bundle everyone up or pick an indoor activity, such as watching a film at the IMAX™ theatre, to get a break from the cold.

Checking Out
THE BANK OF
MONTRÉAL MUSEUM

129 RUE ST-JACQUES O. (ST. JACQUES ST. W.)
MONTRÉAL
(514) 877-6810

The Bank of Montréal Museum is a must see for any future financier. A self-guided tour of the small museum in the bank's impressive-looking former head office takes visitors to the very origins of Canadian banking. Inside you'll see a recreation of the Bank of Montréal's first office, displays of old bank notes, gold and coins and even rare piggy banks. The exhibits recall a time when financial institutions and not governments issued money.

St. Jacques Street was Canada's financial capital during most of Canada's early history, which the Bank of Montréal helped to shape by financing projects such as the Canadian Pacific Railway.

☞ **SEASONS AND TIMES**
➤ Year-round: Mon—Fri, 10 am—3 pm.

☞ **COST**
➤ Free.

☞ **GETTING THERE**
➤ By car, take St. Urbain St. south to St. Jacques St. and turn west the Museum is on the corner.
➤ By public transit, take the metro (orange line) to the Place-d'Armes station. Walk south along St. Urbain St. to St. Jacques St.

☞ **NEARBY**
➤ The Montréal Stock Exchange, Peregrine Falcon Information Centre, Montréal History Museum.

☞ **COMMENT**
➤ Restaurants and cafés in the vicinity. Plan a 30-minute visit. The original head office of the Bank of Montréal on St. Paul St. now houses the doll museum (page 48).

POUPÉES ET MERVEILLES
(Dolls and Treasures)

105 RUE ST-PAUL E. (ST. PAUL ST. E.)
OLD MONTRÉAL
(514) 866-0110 OR 1-888-459-5002

D olls and more dolls. At this museum you'll find a collection comprising nearly 4,000 figures and spanning 120 years. The 500 dolls on view include ones made from celluloid, a highly-flammable precursor to plastic, Barbie and Ken and the latest Lady Diana look-a-likes, all presented in various thematic displays. Small signs (in French only) describe each of the scenes, which

☞ **SEASONS AND TIMES**
➤ Winter: Nov—Dec and Feb—Mar, Thu—Sun, 11 am—6 pm.
Summer: April—Oct, Wed—Mon, 11 am—8 pm.

☞ **COST**
➤ Adults $5, seniors and students $4.50, children (3 to 12) $2.50, under 3 free, families $11. Group rates available.

☞ **GETTING THERE**
➤ By car, take St. Urbain St. south to Notre Dame St., turn east then go south on St. Vincent. Head west on St. Paul St. and continue on to the museum. It's on the right. Pay parking at the lot near Pointe à Callière Museum. It's a five-minute walk from there.
➤ By public transit, take the metro (green line) to the St. Laurent station and transfer to bus 55 going south. Get off at Notre Dame Basilica and walk one block south towards the river to St. Paul St., then one block east.
➤ By bicycle, from the Berri St.-de la Commune-Lachine Canal bike path, go up Place Jacques Cartier from de la Commune St. Turn west onto St. Paul St.

include a general store, a
bakery, Christmas celebrations and others.

While the displays are
too high to be viewed by
tots in strollers, older kids

☞ **NEARBY**
➤ Old Port, Pointe à Callière
Museum

☞ **COMMENT**
➤ Plan a 30-minute visit.

will like their visit. Guided tours are offered to groups.

Other Places to Visit

Notre Dame Basilica

110 RUE NOTRE-DAME O. (NOTRE DAME ST. W.)
(514) 849-1070
PLACE-D'ARMES METRO

While the original chapel dates back to 1642,
construction on the Gothic Revival building
you see today began in 1829. If the sheer size, can-
dles, stained glass and beautiful carved wood don't
impress your kids, tell them this is where Céline
Dion was married. Guided tours are available ($2).

☞ Open year-round. Donations are appreciated.

Bonsecours Market

350 RUE ST-PAUL E. (ST. PAUL ST. E.)
(514) 872-7730
CHAMP-DE-MARS METRO

Built during the middle of the 1800s, Bonsecours
Market originally housed a city hall, a public
market and a reception centre. It's now home to a
farmers' market and artisans' shops and is the site of
various exhibitions throughout the year.

☞ Year-round : Sat—Wed, 10 am—6 pm; Thu—Fri, 10 am—9 pm.

CHAPTER 3

museums

Introduction

For a family outing that's educational and loads of fun, go to one of Montréal's many museums. Most offer a fantastic variety of sights and activities that have been designed with kids in mind. Your children will learn about architecture, history, trains, art, farm tractors, fighting fires and just about everything else as they explore life-size exhibits, take in dynamic displays, watch films, play computer games and participate in interactive activities. Many of the museums also have workshops and courses for kids. If you don't mind the crowds, most Montréal museums offer free admission on Museum Day, generally the last Sunday in May.

This chapter tells you all you need to know about these kid-friendly museums. Choosing among them won't be easy, so you might think of your first outing as just the beginning.

NOTE

The following museums, which are covered elsewhere in this guide, also welcome children.

Biodome	(Chapter 1, page 21)
Insectarium	(Chapter 1, page 33)
Montréal Museum of History	(Chapter 2, page 41)
Pointe-à-Callière Museum	(Chapter 2, page 43)
Bank of Montréal Museum	(Chapter 2, page 47)
Dolls and Treasures	(Chapter 2, page 48)
Armand Frappier Museum	(Chapter 6, page 116)
Musée des Ondes Emile Berliner	(Chapter 6, page 122)
Ecomuseum	(Chapter 8, page 149)
Fur Trade Museum	(Chapter 10, page 185)
Stewart Museum	(Chapter 10, page 196)
J. Armand Bombardier Museum	(Chapter 12, page 226)
Gilles Villeneuve Museum	(Chapter 12, page 230)

Discovering Our Past at
THE McCORD MUSEUM
OF CANADIAN HISTORY

690 RUE SHERBROOKE O. (SHERBROOKE ST. W.)
MONTRÉAL
(514) 398-7100
WWW.MCCORD-MUSEUM.QC.CA

Your whole family can investigate Canadian history at the McCord Museum. In fact students, scholars and writers from across the country regularly visit the museum to reference the nearly 800,000 Canadian artifacts found there. Most of the collection dates from the 1700s to the present, and among the treasures you can view are costumes, textiles, decorative art, photographs, paintings, prints, drawings and aboriginal artifacts. Kids will enjoy the interactive displays and you'll find films and soundtracks throughout the museum.

The McCord also has temporary exhibits that encompass a variety of Canadian themes, ranging from the history of hockey to the aboriginal

☞ **SEASONS AND TIMES**
→ Year-round: Tue—Fri, 10 am—6 pm (Thu until 9 pm); weekends, 10 am—5 pm.

☞ **COST**
→ Adults $8.05, seniors $5.75, children (6 to 12) $1.73, under 6 free, families $16.10.

☞ **GETTING THERE**
→ By car, take Sherbrooke St. to University St. The museum is located on the southwest corner. Finding parking nearby can be difficult.
→ By public transit, take the 24 bus to University St. By metro, take the green line to the McGill station and walk north for two blocks along University St.

☞ **NEARBY**
→ The Montréal Museum of Fine Arts.

☞ **COMMENT**
→ Plan a 1-hour visit.

peoples of early Québec. The McCord Museum offers interactive tours to school groups and there are workshops, lectures, theatre productions and concerts throughout the year. Their Christmas programs are particularly kid-friendly. Ask about these activities at the information desk or call 398-7100 ext. 234.

Gallery Games at THE MONTRÉAL MUSEUM OF FINE ARTS

1380 RUE SHERBROOKE O. (SHERBROOKE ST. W.)
MONTRÉAL
(514) 285-2000
WWW.MMFA.QC.CA

A trip to the Montréal Museum of Fine Arts is a highlight for any art enthusiast. Canada's oldest and arguably most elegant art museum houses an exquisite collection of over 25,000 paintings, sculptures, drawings, photographs and decorative art objects.

But if *making* art sounds more exciting than looking at it, visit the museum during its Sunday family programs when there are guessing and observation games, treasure hunts, storytelling and craftmaking. These activities make it fun for kids of

---

☞ **SEASONS AND TIMES**
➤ Year-round: Tue—Sun, 10 am—7 pm (Wed until 9 pm).

☞ **COST**
➤ Permanent collection: Free. Temporary exhibits: Adults $12, seniors and students $6, children (3 to 12) $3, under 3 free, families $24.

☞ **GETTING THERE**

➤ By car, take Sherbrooke St. west from University St. until Crescent St. Metered parking nearby (free on Sundays).

➤ By public transit, take the metro (green line) to the Guy-Concordia station and exit via Guy St. Walk north for two blocks, cross Sherbrooke St. and head east for three blocks, or take the 24 bus along Sherbrooke.

➤ The museum is about a 10-minute walk from downtown.

☞ **NEARBY**

➤ McCord Museum of Canadian History.

☞ **COMMENT**

➤ Plan a 1-hour visit.

all ages to learn about art. Materials for making art are supplied and the sessions are free.

The museum has workshops for kids ages 6 to 12 and children's birthday party art workshops too. It also offers tours to school groups and has an outreach program designed to introduce children as young as kindergarten age to art. For details, call 285-1600 ext. 136. To arrange a school group tour, call 285-1600 ext. 135 or e-mail nbourcier@mbamtl.org.

Toy Towns at
THE CANADIAN CENTRE FOR ARCHITECTURE

1920 RUE BAILE (BAILE ST.)
MONTRÉAL
(514) 939-7026
WWW.CCA.QC.CA

☞ SEASONS AND TIMES
→ Winter: Oct–May, Wed–Fri,
11 am–6 pm (Thu until 8 pm);
weekends, 11 am–5 pm.
Summer: June–Sept, Tue–Sun,
11 am–6 pm (Thu until 9 pm).
Weekend Workshops: Nov–April,
11 am and 2 pm. Register three weeks
in advance.

☞ COST
→ Adults $6, seniors $4, students
and children $3, under 6 free, fami-
lies $15.
Students free all day Thursday.
Weekend Workshops: Adults $4,
children $2.

☞ GETTING THERE
→ By car, take de Maisonneuve Blvd.
west and turn south on du Fort St.
until Baile St. Limited free parking.
→ By public transit, take the metro
(green line) to the Guy-Concordia
station and exit via St. Mathieu St.
and walk south for three blocks.
→ On foot, about a 10-minute walk
from downtown.

Weekends are a special time for families at the Canadian Centre for Architecture. That's when children's activities, including toy-making workshops, take place. Sometimes budding architects can even construct miniature towns.

Another reason for the centre's popularity is the stunning architectural exhibits, both permanent and temporary, displayed inside the beautifully restored Shaughnessy House. Wander around the old manor and the new building, and visit the library, theatre and bookstore. Outside, there's an urban garden and outdoor museum.

> ☞ **COMMENT**
> ➤ Plan a 45-minute visit.

Remember to take your kids to see the current exhibition, and the play sessions organized around it. Call 939-7026 for scheduling information. School groups can register for two-hour winter workshops by calling 939-7002.

All Aboard for THE CANADIAN RAILWAY MUSEUM

122-A RUE ST-PIERRE (ST. PIERRE ST.)
ST-CONSTANT
(450) 632-2410 (RECORDING) OR (450) 638-1522
WWW.EXPORAIL.ORG/MUSEE/MUSEE_CRM.HTM

Where do great Canadian trains go when they reach the end of the line? To the Canadian Railway Museum, where more than 130 locomotives, cabooses and other railroad vehicles are on display.

Some of the equipment is still operational and you can ride aboard a steam locomotive or hop on a tram car and tour the museum's expansive grounds in style. Watch trainmen jump from moving engines and throw

> ☞ **SEASONS AND TIMES**
> ➤ Summer: May—Aug, daily, 9 am—5 pm.
> Fall: Sept—Oct, Sat—Sun, 9 am—5 pm.
> Reservations required on weekdays.
>
> ☞ **COST**
> ➤ Adults $6, seniors $5, students $4, children $3, under 6 free, families $15.

☞ **GETTING THERE**

➜ By car, take the Champlain Bridge south to Hwy.15 S. and continue on to Rte. 132 W. Take it west to Ste. Catherine, then exit south on St. Pierre St. and after two minutes look for the museum on the left (east side of street). Free parking on site. About 30 minutes from downtown.

➜ By public transit, call CIT Roussillon (450-638-2031) for information.

☞ **NEARBY**

➜ Écomusée in St. Constant, Ste. Catherine beach.

☞ **COMMENT**

➜ Plan a 90-minute visit.

track switches to keep the trains on time.

More rolling stock is parked inside giant hangars and can be boarded for inspection. The size of some of the engines is unbelievable! Or, head to the telegraph office where kids can practise Morse code on a telegraph machine.

Visits from school groups are welcome, as the museum has educational programs that cater to everyone from tots to teens. Call for reservations or more information.

Picnicking by
THE FLEMING MILL

9675 BOUL. LASALLE (LASALLE BLVD.)
LASALLE
(514) 367-6439

I f you want your kids to experience a piece of Québec history, visit the Fleming Mill. The windmill has been restored—it's not operational—to appear as it did 150 years ago when William Fleming milled farmers' wheat to make flour, a privilege reserved for the Sulpicians.

☞ **SEASONS AND TIMES**
➤ Summer: May—Aug, Sat—Sun, 1 pm—5 pm.
Call ahead for group visits – 367-6489.

☞ **COST**
➤ Free.

☞ **GETTING THERE**
➤ By car, take Hwy. 720 W. to Hwy. 15 S. and continue to de la Vérendrye Blvd. (Exit 62). Turn south on de l'Église Ave., west on Champlain Blvd. and continue to LaSalle Blvd. Turn north on LaSalle and follow it until Strathyre Ave. Free parking on site. About 25 minutes from downtown.
➤ By public transit, take the metro (green line) to the Angrignon station and transfer to buses 110, 106, or 114. It's a long ride.
➤ By bicycle, follow the LaSalle Blvd. bicycle path to the windmill.

☞ **NEARBY**
➤ Lachine Canal bicycle path, René Lévesque Park, Lachine Outdoor Museum, Fur Trade Museum.

☞ **COMMENT**
➤The windmill is not wheelchair/stroller accessible, however, the park is. Bilingual guides, but French-only signs.

☞ **SIMILAR ATTRACTION**
➤ **Pointe du Moulin Park**
2500 boul. Don Quichotte (Don Quixote Blvd.)
Île-Perrot
(514) 453-5936

Visit this restored working windmill that dates from 1708. Hands-on exhibits, actors in period costumes, guided tours, picnic sites. About 45 minutes from downtown. Free admission to the park and site.

Summer: Mid-May—early Sept, daily, 9 am—6 pm.
Fall: Early Sept—Thanksgiving, Sat—Sun and holidays,12 noon—6 pm.

Step inside and let the miller, an actor in period costume, show you around. Watch audio and visual displays about area life during the early 1800s in the interpretive centre. While some of the displays are hands-on, most are narrative.

Pick a nice day for your visit and pack a lunch. The picnic area offers a spectacular view of the St. Lawrence River and the Seaway. There are washrooms across Strathyre Avenue if anyone needs one.

Visiting
THE FIREFIGHTER'S MUSEUM

BOUL. ST-LAURENT AND AV. LAURIER
(ST. LAURENT BLVD. AND LAURIER AVE.)
MONTRÉAL
(514) 872-3757

At one time, insurance companies provided fire brigade services to their policy holders with paid-up home insurance. If a burning house did not display the insurance company's crest, it was left to go up in flames. Thankfully, to-day fire departments are a municipal service available to everyone.

You'll learn more fire-fighting lore during your visit to the Firefighter's Museum where there's an impressive collection of firefighters' memorabilia to view. Some of the exhibits date to Montréal's first fire brigade. There are all types of helmets, fire alarms, pumps and extinguishers for examining—from the earliest models to present-day designs. The

☞ **SEASONS AND TIMES**
➤ Year-round: Sun, 2 pm—5 pm.

☞ **COST**
➤ Free (donation requested).

model fire engine display includes pumpers, ladder trucks and every other kind of fire vehicle imaginable. You'll see trophies won by Montréal's firefighters in competitions and photographs that present poignant scenes—some are tender, others are horrific—of fires in Montréal.

☞ **GETTING THERE**

➥ By car, take St. Laurent Blvd. north to Laurier Ave. The museum is located in the fire station at the corner. Metered parking is available on nearby streets and is free on Sundays. About 10 minutes from downtown.

➥ By public transit, take the metro (orange line) to the Laurier station. It's about a 10-minute walk to the museum from there. The museum is served by the 51 and 55 buses.

☞ **COMMENT**

➥ Volunteer operated—primarily by retired firefighters. Bilingual signs, but tour guides may be unilingual French speaking. Restaurants nearby. Plan a 30-minute visit.

Science Workshops at THE REDPATH MUSEUM

859 RUE SHERBROOKE O. ON THE MCGILL UNIVERSITY CAMPUS
(SHERBROOKE ST. W.)
MONTRÉAL
(514) 398-4086
WWW.MCGILL.CA/REDPATH

W hy was a whale skeleton unearthed in Montréal and what's the connection to apple growing? You'll learn the answer to this and other conundrums at the Redpath Museum.

Guide yourself through this classic science museum that features narrative displays about biology, palaeontology, geology and Egyptology. Discover fossils, see a life-size dinosaur skeleton, and come face to face with a real mummy. Rock hounds will love the exten-

→ Winter: Sept—June, Mon—Fri,
9 am—5 pm; Sun, 1 pm—5 pm.
Summer: June—Sept, Mon—Thu,
9 am—5 pm; Sun, 1 pm—5 pm.

☞ **COST**
→ Free. Fees for special events.

☞ **GETTING THERE**
→ By car, take Sherbrooke St. to
McGill College Ave. Parking is hard
to find on campus but metered parking is available on Sherbrooke.
→ By public transit, take the 24 bus
along Sherbrooke St. to McGill
College Ave. Or, take the metro
(green line) to the McGill station,
exit via McGill College Ave. and walk
north for two blocks. The gates to the
campus are on the north side of
Sherbrooke. The security guard will
direct you to the museum.

☞ **NEARBY**
→ The McCord Museum

☞ **COMMENT**
→ Lots of stairs inside. Few facilities on
site, but a cafeteria, telephones and
grassy fields for picnics can be found
on campus. Plan a 1-hour visit.

sive mineral collection.
Also on display are taxi-
dermal animals, birds'
eggs, mounted insects and
mastodon bones.

The museum hosts
Sunday workshops (main-
ly in English, but additional French sessions are
under development) to in-
troduce young children to
science. There's a one-
hour session at 2 pm for
children 4 to 7, and another for kids 8 to 12 years old
at 3:30 pm. A $5 fee covers
material costs and reser-
vations are required.
School tours for kids as
young as 4 can be arranged.
For more information, call
398-4086 ext. 4092 from
Tuesday to Thursday.

Learning about Geology at
THE ÉCOMUSÉE

66 RUE MAÇON (MAÇON ST.)
ST-CONSTANT
(450) 632-3656

A visit to this earth science museum will satisfy anyone with questions about geology. You can explore the site on your own or go on a guided tour and view fossils of long-extinct plants and animals, models of dinosaurs and dazzling collections of precious gems and gold. You'll even learn why volcanoes erupt, and all about fault zones. Bilingual signs accompany each of the exhibits.

Most of the displays are narrative and suited for school-age children, however younger kids will still enjoy their visit. They can play nature bingo and other environmental awareness games, or go on a safari on the grounds. Outside, you'll find nature trails for exploring and there is a pond and a community garden.

☞ **SEASONS AND TIMES**
➤ Winter: Sept—April, Sat—Sun, 10 am—7 pm.
Summer: May—Aug, Mon—Fri, 9 am—5 pm; Sat—Sun, 10 am—7 pm.
Closed holidays.

☞ **COST**
➤ Adults $3, children $3, under 6 free.

☞ **GETTING THERE**
➤ By car, take Hwy. 20 W. to Hwy. 138 S. and cross the Mercier Bridge. Access Hwy. 132 E. and follow it to Maçon St. (the first light after the Hwy. 30 junction) then turn south. There are posted signs to the museum. Free parking on site. About 35 minutes from downtown.
By public transit, call CIT Roussillon (450-638-2031) for information.

☞ **NEARBY**
➤ The Canadian Railway Museum.

☞ **COMMENT**
➤ Gravel paths around the site make it difficult to push strollers. Plan a 90-minute visit.

Riding Tractors at AUX COULEURS DE LA CAMPAGNE *(Agricultural Museum)*

2864 RTE. 219
ACADIE
(450) 346-1630

H obby farmers will revel at the sight of this much farm machinery. But if tractors don't excite your youngsters, a visit to the playground at this agricultural museum certainly will. It features slides, swings and teeter-totters, all made out of tractor parts. Your kids can also see chickens, rabbits and other farm animals.

The main attraction for adults, however, will be the collection of completely restored farm tractors and other agricultural machinery on display outdoors. Collecting farm equipment began as a hobby for Mr. Bertrand, the museum's owner—until he had amassed 400 machines. Needing

☞ **SEASONS AND TIMES**
➤ Summer: Late June—Labour Day, Wed—Sun, 10 am—5 pm.
Fall: Sept—Oct, Sat—Sun, 1 pm—5 pm.
Group visits possible during other months.

☞ **COST**
➤ Adults $5, seniors and students $4, children (6 to 12) $2, under 6 free, families $12.

☞ **GETTING THERE**
➤ By car, take Hwy. 15 S. to Exit 21. Turn east and follow the signs for Napierville. In Napierville, turn north on Rte. 219 and continue on to the farm. Free parking on site. About 50 minutes from downtown.

☞ **NEARBY**
➤ Il était une fois . . . une petite colonie.

☞ **COMMENT**
➤ Plan a 90-minute visit.

more room, he bought the farm and then started the museum.

The site combines educational activities and fun times, such as learning about farming practices while going for a tractor ride. The variety of farm machinery is fascinating to see, but keep your kids close-by for safety's sake. Most of the equipment can be started by pushing a button.

Other Museums

Just for Laughs Museum

2111 BOUL. ST-LAURENT (ST. LAURENT BLVD.)
MONTRÉAL
(514) 845-4000
WWW.HAHAHA.COM
ST-LAURENT METRO

This museum devoted to humour features a Hall of Fame of great humourists, karaoke, a video café and numerous temporary exhibits. Sometimes the museum is closed while preparing for new exhibits. Call to make sure it's open before visiting.

☞ Year-round: Tue—Sun, 10 am—5 pm.

☞ Adults $5, children (12 and under) $3.

Marsil Museum

349 RUE RIVERSIDE (RIVERSIDE ST.)
ST-LAMBERT
(450) 583-3191

T his museum dedicated to costume, textiles and fibres hosts bilingual children's workshops on Sundays between 2 and 4 pm (included in admission) and also has costumes to try on. School visits are available. Reservations required.

☞ Year-round: Tue—Fri, 10 am—4 pm; weekends, 1—4 pm.

☞ Adults $2, seniors and students $1, children under 12 free.

☞ Take Hwy. 20 E. and cross the Champlain Bridge to Exit 6 (Riverside). Go east on Riverside to the corner of Notre-Dame. Free parking on street and at municipal park across the street. Take the metro (orange line) to Longueuil, then take STRS buses 6, 13 or 15.

Lachine Canal Interpretation Centre

CORNER OF 7E AVE. AND BOUL. ST-JOSEPH (7TH AVE. AND ST. JOSEPH'S BLVD.)
LACHINE
(514) 637-7433 OR 283-6054
ANGRIGNON METRO AND 195 BUS WEST

L ocated near the western terminus of the Lachine Canal, the interpretation centre has exhibits that detail the construction and history of the waterway vital to Montréal's early development.

☞ Mid-May—Labour Day, daily, 10 am—noon, 1 pm—6 pm. Closed Monday mornings.

☞ Free.

Montréal Museum of Contemporary Art

185 RUE STE-CATHERINE O. (ST. CATHERINE ST. W.)
MONTRÉAL
(514) 847-6226
WWW.MACM.ORG
PLACE-DES-ARTS METRO

This museum features educational activities, multimedia creations, experimental theatre, modern dance, music, video and film. Don't forget to check out the waterfall at the front door.

School groups and daycare centres can sign up for the museum's popular art workshops held during the school year (best to reserve before Labour Day) by calling 847-6253 or e-mailing davidsophie@macm.org. Prices start at $1 per student for a one-hour session. In addition, the museum runs an art camp and Sunday afternoon workshops for children ages 4 to 14. Birthday parties can also be arranged. For more information, call 847-6253.

☞ Year-round: Tue—Sun, 11 am—6 pm (Wed until 9 pm).

☞ Adults $6, seniors $4, students $3, children under 12 free, families $12. Free on Wednesdays after 6 pm.

The World of Maurice "Rocket" Richard

MAURICE RICHARD ARENA
2800 RUE VIAU (VIAU ST.)
MONTRÉAL
(514) 251-9930
WWW.TOURISMEMAISONNEUVE.QC.CA
VIAU METRO

E xhibits about the life and times of one of
Canada's greatest hockey players at the Maurice
Richard Arena next to the Olympic Park.

☞ Year-round: Tue—Sun, noon—6 pm.

☞ Admission to the museum is free.

CHAPTER 4

In Your
Neighbourhood

Introduction

S ometimes you don't need to travel far to find attractions and activities that will interest kids. Many of the best places to take children are in your own neighbourhood, and most cost very little or are free.

This chapter contains a variety of ideas for outings to public markets, bowling alleys, craft shops and other everyday places, where a little imagination can turn even an ordinary trip into a fun-filled adventure. Have you ever thought about taking your kids to visit the local fire station? They'll love it. The telephone numbers and addresses of these and other neighbourhood attractions, including pools, rinks and children's libraries, are provided on the following pages. There's also a listing of some of Montréal's more popular and inexpensive family restaurants, as well as the names of children's haircutters that will not only make your kids look good, but keep them amused while they're at it.

Places to Paint
YOUR OWN POTTERY

I f your kids need a new medium for expressing their artistic side, take them to a café where they can paint pottery. You can purchase cups, bowls, piggy banks or a variety of ceramic figures, with prices starting at $7 for some of the smaller items. The café supplies the paints and brushes, and voila!, your children will be occupied creatively for an hour or two.

But you'd better put a limit on the number of pieces you're prepared to buy; younger painters tend to finish their chef-d'oeuvres quickly and want to do more. It can get expensive. The café will fire the pottery and you can drop by in a day or two to pick it up.

CÉRAMIC CAFÉ-STUDIO INC.
4201-B RUE ST-DENIS, MONTRÉAL • (514) 848-1119
95 RUE DE LA COMMUNE E., MONTRÉAL • (514) 868-1611

CAFÉ ART FOLIE
5511 AV. MONKLAND, MONTRÉAL • (514) 487-6066
3339-C BOUL. DE SOURCES, DOLLARD-DES-ORMEAUX • (514) 685-1980

ATELIER LA FORÊT
19 AV. CARTIER, POINTE-CLAIRE • (514) 697-3737

POTERIE CAFÉ
450-B BOUL. BEACONSFIELD, BEACONSFIELD • (514) 697-8187

CAFÉ CERAMIQUE
6925 BOUL. TASCHERAU, BROSSARD • (450) 443-8582

Rainy Day
BOWLING ALLEYS

Bowling is an ideal rainy-day activity for kids and their parents. Children as young as two will enjoy playing, albeit by their own rules. Certain alleys in the area cater to families by making lightweight, easy-to-handle balls available to children. At other establishments kids can bowl on bumper lanes (lanes with no gutters), guaranteeing they'll hit the pins every time. Mornings are usually the best time to take the family bowling; the alleys are less crowded then and not as smoky.

☞ **SEASONS AND TIMES**
➤ Year-round: Daily.

☞ **COST**
➤ One game: $2 to $3 per person.
Shoe rental: $1.50 per pair.
Birthday packages: Inquire at the alley.

If your kids enjoy the sport—a game between four friends lasts about 45 minutes—they might want to celebrate their birthdays at the lanes. Staff will tell you what facilities are available for children's parties. Birthday packages may include several games of bowling, shoe rentals, a lunch, a decorated birthday room and balloons.

There's no shortage of bowling alleys in the Montréal area. Here's a selection of those offering children's birthday parties:

ROSEBOWL
6510 RUE ST-JACQUES, MONTRÉAL • (514) 482-7200

LE FORUM
920 RUE ST-ZOTIQUE, MONTRÉAL • (514) 274-0797

SPOT
12255 RUE GRENET, ST-LAURENT • (514) 334-7881

LA SALLE
1277 BOUL. SHEVCHENKO, LASALLE • (514) 366-5105

BANNANTYNE
5146 RUE BANNANTYNE, VERDUN • (514) 761-1422

VILLE ÉMARD
2585 RUE ALLARD, MONTRÉAL • (514) 761-5887

MASCOUCHE
930 MTÉE MASSON, LACHENAIE • (450) 474-6711

REPENTIGNY
130 BOUL. INDUSTRIEL, REPENTIGNY • (450) 585-8474

LE RIVERAIN
6280 ST-LAURENT, STE-CATHERINE • (450) 635-0660

Shopping at a
PUBLIC MARKET

WWW.MARCHESPUBLICS-MTL.COM

The next time you need to shop for fruits and vegetables, consider buying them at a public market. These open-air emporiums offer children the sights and smells of fresh farm produce amidst the hustle and bustle of commercial activity.

While the cost of potatoes, cucumbers, strawberries and other fruits grown by area farmers generally matches supermarket prices, there's no comparing the quality of goods or the atmosphere.

☞ **SEASONS AND TIMES**
→ Year-round: Mon—Wed, 7 am— 6 pm; Thu—Fri, 7 am—9 pm; weekends, 7 am—5 pm. Special activities usually happen in late summer and early fall.

☞ **COST**
→ Free to browse. Parking charges may apply.

☞ **COMMENT**
→ Toilets are not usually available at public markets. Keep an eye open for nearby restaurants.

You can purchase in-season firewood, maple syrup, Halloween pumpkins and Christmas trees at year-round markets and some have seasonal activities. Don't miss the strawberry and ice cream party at the Maisonneuve market in June or the corn roast that's held every August at the Jean Talon market.

ATWATER MARKET
138 AV. ATWATER, MONTRÉAL • (514) 935-5716

JEAN-TALON MARKET
7075 AV. CASGRAIN, MONTRÉAL • (514) 277-1873

LACHINE MARKET
18ᴱ AV. & RUE NOTRE-DAME, LACHINE • (514) 634-3471

MAISONNEUVE MARKET
4445 RUE ONTARIO E., MONTRÉAL • (514) 253-3993

MARCHÉ DE L'OUEST
11600 RUE DE SALABERRY, DOLLARD-DES-ORMEAUX • (514) 333-8974

MARCHÉ CENTRAL
BOUL. CRÉMAZIE & BOUL. DE L'ACADIE, MONTRÉAL • (514) 381-7219

MARCHÉ PUBLIC
440 3535 AUTOROUTE 440, LAVAL • (450) 682-1440

Visiting the Neighbourhood
FIRE STATION

Firefighters like showing kids around their stations. Not every station house has a fireman's pole but children will get to see gleaming trucks, rescue equipment, uniforms and other firefighting paraphernalia. Officials from fire departments often give talks to daycares and school groups about fire prevention. A visit to a station house makes a terrific follow-up. In Montréal, call

872-3800 for more information. Elsewhere, look in the blue pages for the administration number (not the emergency number) of your municipal department. Some stations have a fire prevention colouring book for children who visit, published by the Québec Association of Fire Chiefs.

☞ **SEASONS AND TIMES**
→ Call your municipal fire department for information.

☞ **COST**
→ Free.

☞ **COMMENT**
→ Call ahead to see if your visit will be at a convenient time.

Dining Out at KID-FRIENDLY RESTAURANTS

D ining out with the family offers two rewards: it's fun and it gives the cook in the household a well-deserved break. But if you have many mouths to feed, it can be expensive. Fortunately, there's no shortage of family restaurants in the Montréal area where diners can choose from a variety of dishes and expect good value. Better still, these establishments are happy to see kids. Many have children's menus and serve kiddie-size portions. Others provide crayons or offer activities to keep the little ones happy. But before heading out with the troops, call ahead to ask if the restaurant has high-chairs or child boosters.

BAR-B-BARN
(KIDS' MENUS, CRAYONS)
1201 RUE GUY, MONTRÉAL • (514) 931-3811
3300 BOUL. DES SOURCES, POINTE-CLAIRE • (514) 683-0225

BARBIE'S RESTAURANT
(KIDS' MENU)
15 BOUL. BOUCHARD, DORVAL • (514) 631-2233

BEN & JERRY'S
(THIS BRANCH OF THE POPULAR ICE CREAM PLACES OFFERS CHILDREN'S BIRTHDAY PARTIES.
KIDS CAN MAKE THEIR OWN ICE CREAM AND TIE-DYED SHIRTS.)
5582 AV. MONKLAND, MONTRÉAL • (514) 488-6524

CHEZ GATSÉ
(TIBETAN FOOD)
317 RUE ONTARIO E., MONTRÉAL • (514) 985-2494

LE COMMENSAL
(SELF-SERVE VEGETARIAN RESTAURANTS)
1720 RUE ST-DENIS, MONTRÉAL • (514) 845-2627
1204 AV. MCGILL COLLEGE, MONTRÉAL • (514) 871-1480
3715 CH. QUEEN MARY, MONTRÉAL • (514) 733-9755
5043 RUE ST-DENIS, MONTRÉAL • (514) 843-7741
2170 RUE STE-CATHERINE O., MONTRÉAL • (514) 846-0888
360 PL. SICARD, STE-THÉRÈSE • (450) 433-0505
3180 BOUL. ST.-MARTIN O., CHOMEDEY • (450) 978-9124

À LA CRÉPE BRETONNE
5058 AV. DU PARC, MONTRÉAL • (514) 278-3353

DA GIOVANNI
572 RUE STE-CATHERINE E., MONTRÉAL • (514) 842-8851
6835 BOUL. TASCHEREAU, BROSSARD • (450) 678-5533

JACK ASTOR'S BAR & GRILL
(KIDS' MENUS)
3051 BOUL. DES SOURCES, DORVAL • (514) 685-5225
3556 BOUL. TASCHEREAU, GREENFIELD PARK • (450) 671-4444

JARDIN SAKURA
(SUSHI)
2114 RUE DE LA MONTAGNE, MONTRÉAL • (514) 288-9122

KATSURA RESTAURANT
(WATCH SUSHI BEING MADE)
2170 RUE DE LA MONTAGNE, MONTRÉAL • (514) 849-1172

MOISHE'S STEAK HOUSE
(SERVES SHIRLEY TEMPLES AND BUBBLE GUM)
3961 BOUL. ST-LAURENT, MONTRÉAL • (514) 845-3509

PIZZEDELIC

(THE MOUNT ROYAL AND MONKLAND BRANCHES WEIGH YOUR KID IN A CHAIR TO
DETERMINE HOW MUCH TO CHARGE)

3503 BOUL. ST-LAURENT, MONTRÉAL • (514) 282-6784
1329 RUE STE-CATHERINE E., MONTRÉAL • (514) 526-6011
370 AV. LAURIER O., MONTRÉAL • (514) 948-6290
1250 AV. DU MONT-ROYAL E., MONTRÉAL • (514) 522-2286
5153 CH. DE LA CÔTE-DES-NEIGES, MONTRÉAL • (514) 739-2446
5556 AV. MONKLAND, MONTRÉAL • (514) 487-3103

ST-HUBERT'S

(THESE BRANCHES HAVE KIDS' ACTIVITY ROOMS, $1.99 KIDS' MEAL AFTER 4 PM ON
TUESDAYS, CRAYONS AND BIRTHDAY PARTIES.)

665 AV. 32IEME, LACHINE
10495 BOUL. PIE IX, MONTRÉAL
6415 RUE SHERBROOKE O., MONTRÉAL
7870 RUE SHERBROOKE E, MONTRÉAL
12575 RUE SHERBROOKE STREET E, POINTE-AUX-TREMBLES (MONTRÉAL)
2901 RUE SHERBROOKE STREET E, MONTRÉAL
6355 RUE ST-HUBERT, MONTRÉAL
4700 BOUL. ST-JEAN, PIERREFONDS
1111 BOUL. DES LAURENTIDES, LAVAL
1963 BOUL. DES LAURENTIDES, LAVAL
3325 BOUL. ST-MARTIN O, LAVAL
500 BOUL. STE-ADELE, STE-ADELE
555 BOUL. SAUVÉ, ST-EUSTACHE
350 BOUL. LABELLE, STE-THÉRÈSE
1415 BOUL. MOODY, TERREBONNE
91 BOUL. LAURIER, BELOEIL
500 RUE ALBANEL, BOUCHERVILLE
8 BOUL. BROMONT, BROMONT
107 CH. ST-FRANÇOIS-XAVIER, CANDIAC
940 RUE PRINCIPALE, GRANBY
825 RUE ST-LAWRENCE O., LONGUEUIL
1250 RUE GAUVIN, ST-HYACINTHE
435 BOUL. HARWOOD, VAUDREUIL-DORION

VILLA DU SOUVLAKI

5347 RUE SHERBROOKE O., MONTRÉAL • (514) 489-2039

If you're looking for something a bit different, why
not try a buffet? Kids love to choose their own dishes.

BUFFET CHINOIS MANDARIN

1240 RUE STANLEY, MONTRÉAL • (514) 871-8099

BUFFET BAR KIM FOO

990 RUE ST-ANTOINE O., MONTRÉAL • (514) 871-1515
6690 RUE ST-JACQUES O., MONTRÉAL • (514) 487-1515

BUFFET MAHARAJA

1481 BOUL. RENÉ-LÉVESQUE O., MONTRÉAL • (514) 934-0655

These popular fast food restaurants are located throughout the Montréal area. Make it a Saturday morning tradition or a "kids' night out" treat and stroll to the franchise nearest you!

LA BELLE PROVINCE
(BREAKFAST UNTIL 11 AM WEEKDAYS AND 2 PM WEEKENDS, KIDS' MENUS)

BURGER KING

CHEZ CORA'S
(BREAKFAST RESTAURANT)

HARVEY'S

KENTUCKY FRIED CHICKEN (POULET FRIT KENTUCKY)

LES RESTAURANTS D LAFLEUR INC.
(KIDS' MENUS)

PACINI'S RESTAURANT
(KIDS' MENUS, TOAST YOUR OWN BREAD)

PIZZA HUT
(MAKE YOUR OWN PIZZAS, SUNDAES, KIDS EAT FREE ON TUESDAYS)

McDONALD'S
(PARTIAL LISTING ON PAGE 106)

MIKE'S
(CRAYONS, KIDS' MENUS)

NICKELS
(DINER-STYLE)

SUBWAY

SWISS CHALET

Child's Play
TOY LIBRARIES

There's all kinds of playthings that children can borrow at a toy library. They'll find stuffed animals, games, puzzles and educational toys but there are other items too, such as strollers, highchairs and children's car seats. Some toy libraries also loan out books, clothing, videos and sports equipment.

These establishments operate like regular libraries do; simply wander in and pick out the item or items you wish to borrow and present your membership card at the circulation desk. Loans are generally for two weeks. Many toy libraries have used toys for sale and will accept donations of old toys. Prices are reasonable and each item has been cleaned and repaired.

> ☞ **SEASONS AND TIMES**
> ➜ Year-round: Call for opening hours.
>
> ☞ **COST**
> ➜ Annual membership fees range between $3 and $20. Possible additional user fees.

To borrow records, tapes and compact disks, head to the Phonothèque, the City of Montréal's music library. You'll need to bring a piece of identification proving that you're a resident of the city. The Phonothèque is located at 880 rue Roy E. For more information, call (514) 872-2860.

JOUJOUTHÈQUE BORDEAUX CARTIER
2005 RUE VICTOR-DORÉ, MONTRÉAL • (514) 332-6552

JOUJOUTHÈQUE CÔTE-DES-NEIGES
3600 AV. BARCLAY, MONTRÉAL • (514) 341-2844

JOUJOUTHÈQUE HOCHELAGA-MAISONNEUVE
3946 RUE ADAM, MONTRÉAL • (514) 523-6501

JOUJOUTHÈQUE ROSEMONT
5675 RUE LAFOND, MONTRÉAL • (514) 722-1851

JOUJOUTHÈQUE SAINT-MICHEL
9480 RUE IRÈNE-JOLY, MONTRÉAL • (514) 381-9974

WEST ISLAND TOY LIBRARY
183 RUE DES ÉRABLES, LACHINE • (514) 368-5667

JOUJOUTHÈQUE YMCA ST-LAURENT
1600 RUE CREVIER, MONTRÉAL • (514) 744-6268

JOUJOUTHÈQUE ST-HUBERT
3625 MONTÉE ST-HUBERT, ST-HUBERT • (450) 678-6038

Combing the Area for
CHILDREN'S
HAIRCUTTERS

F or some children, having a first haircut can be as upsetting as visiting the doctor or dentist. But you can turn those pouts into shouts of joy by taking your kids to a children's haircutter. The staff are friendly and your kids will love the games and toys on hand. When your child's turn arrives, he or she will get to sit in a model racing car while their hair is trimmed— there are no barber's chairs or boosters here.

These establishments specialize in cutting children's hair, typically catering to those 11 and under.

MINIMOD COIFFURE INC.
6900 BOUL. DÉCARIE, MONTRÉAL • (514) 733-2040
2305 CH. ROCKLAND, T.M.R • (514) 739-0071
COMPLEXE POINTE-CLAIRE, POINTE-CLAIRE • (514) 694-0535
2600 BOUL. DANIEL-JOHNSON, CHOMEDY • (450) 682-8070
5155 BOUL. LA GRANDE-ALLÉE, BROSSARD • (450) 926-2056

SALON NI-MO
5516 AV. MONKLAND, MONTRÉAL • (514) 484-9566

Local Treasure Chests
CHILDREN'S LIBRARIES

V isit any municipal library and you'll find a children's section. These days they contain more than books and cosy corners. Your kids will also have access to games, toys, videos, music, interactive computers and Internet facilities. In many neighbourhoods you'll be able to choose from an extensive collection of English and French titles, and sometimes books in other languages are available as well. If the library doesn't have a copy of the book your child wants, make an acquisition request at the main desk or ask if they can obtain it on inter-library loan. Many libraries have storytime and other programs for children. Only residents have book-borrowing privileges and can use the audio-visual and computer facilities. Non-residents can use the books in the library.

☞ **SEASONS AND TIMES**
➤ Schedules vary. Some smaller libraries are open just a few days each week.

☞ **COST**
➤ Usually free for residents. Proof of residency may be required—a Hydro bill or driver's license will suffice.

ANJOU
7500 AV. GONCOURT • (450) 493-8260

BEACONSFIELD
303 BOUL. BEACONSFIELD • (514) 428-4460

BOUCHERVILLE
501 CH. DU LAC • (450) 449-8209

CANDIAC
4 BOUL. MONTCALM S. • (450) 444-6030
WWW3.SYMPATICO.CA/BIBLIO.CANDIAC

CHÂTEAUGUAY
15 BOUL. MAPLE • (450) 698-3080

CÔTE-ST-LUC
5851 BOUL. CAVENDISH • (514) 485-6900

DELSON
1 AV. 1 • (450) 638-2542

DOLLARD-DES-ORMEAUX
12001 RUE DE SALABERRY • (514) 684-1496

DORVAL
1401 CH. BORD-DU-LAC • (514) 633-4170

ÎLE-BIZARD
500 RUE DE L'ÉGLISE • (514) 620-6331 EX. 142

KIRKLAND
17100 BOUL. HYMUS • (514) 694-4100

LACHINE
3100 RUE ST-ANTOINE • (514) 634-3471 EX. 546
(KIDS' SECTION CLOSED BETWEEN NOON AND 3 PM.)

LACHINE
(ST-PIERRE BRANCH)
183 RUE DES ÉRABLES • (514) 368-5740

LAPRAIRIE
500 RUE ST-LAURENT • (450) 444-6710
(CLOSED WEDNESDAYS.)

LASALLE
1080 AV. DOLLARD • (514) 367-6376

LAVAL
1535 BOUL. CHOMEDEY • (450) 978-5990

LONGUEUIL
100 RUE ST-LAURENT O. • (450) 646-6700

MONTRÉAL
WWW.VILLE.MONTREAL.QC.CA/BIBLIO

CENTRALE	2225 RUE MONTCALM	(514) 872-1633
ACADIE	11833 BOUL. DE L'ACADIE	(514) 872-6989
AHUNTSIC	798 BOUL. HENRI-BOURASSA E.	(514) 872-6994
BENNY	3475 AV. BENNY	(514) 872-4636
CÔTE-DES-NEIGES	5290 CH. DE LA CÔTE-DES-NEIGES	(514) 872-5118
(CLOSED FOR RENOVATIONS AT TIME OF PRINTING.)		
FRONTENAC	2550 RUE ONTARIO E.	(514) 872-7888
GEORGES-VANIER	530 RUE VINET	(514) 872-2002
HOCHELAGA	1870 RUE DAVIDSON	(514) 872-3666
LANGELIER	6473 RUE SHERBROOKE E.	(514) 872-4227

LE PRÉVOST	7355 AV. CHRISTOPHE COLOMB	(514) 872-1526
MAISONNEUVE	4120 RUE ONTARIO E.	(514) 872-4214
MARIE-UGUAY	6052 BOUL. MONK	(514) 872-4414
MILE END	5434 AV. DU PARC	(514) 872-2142
NOTRE-DAME	4700 RUE NOTRE-DAME O.	(514) 872-4698
NOTRE-DAME-DE-GRÂCE	3755 RUE BOTREL	(514) 872-2377
PLATEAU MONT-ROYAL	465 AV. DU MONT-ROYAL E.	(514) 872-2271
POINTE-AUX-TREMBLES	14001 RUE NOTRE-DAME E.	(514) 872-6987
RIVIÈRES-DES-PRAIRIES	9001 BOUL. PERRAS	(514) 872-9494
ROSEMONT	3131 BOUL. ROSEMONT	(514) 872-6139
ST-CHARLES	1050 RUE HIBERNIA	(514) 872-3035
ST-MICHEL	7601 RUE FRANÇOIS-PERRAULT	(514) 872-4250
SALABERRY	4170 RUE DE SALABERRY	(514) 872-1521

MONTRÉAL EAST
11370 RUE NOTRE-DAME E. • (514) 645-7431 EX. 272
WWW.VILLE.MONTREAL-EST.QC.CA

MONTRÉAL NORTH
5400 BOUL. HENRI-BOURASSA E. • (514) 328-4125

MONTRÉAL WEST
314 RUE NORTHVIEW • (514) 484-7194

OUTREMONT
41 AV. ST-JUST • (514) 495-6208

PIERREFONDS
13555 BOUL. PIERREFONDS • (514) 620-4181

POINTE-CLAIRE
100 AV. DOUGLAS-SHAND • (514) 630-1218

REPENTIGNY
1 PLACE D'EVRY • (450) 654-2345

ROXBORO
110 RUE CARTIER • (514) 684-8247

STE-ANNE-DE-BELLEVUE
60 BOUL. ST-PIERRE • (514) 457-1940
(CLOSED FRIDAY AND SUNDAY.)

STE-CATHERINE
5365 BOUL. ST-LAURENT • (450) 632-9951

ST-CONSTANT
80 RUE BRODEUR • (450) 632-8732

ST-HUBERT
5245 BOUL. COUSINEAU • (450) 445-7761

ST-LAMBERT MAIN
490 AV. MERCILLE • (450) 923-6500

St-Lambert Annex
120 rue de Poitou • (450) 923-6510

St-Laurent
1380 rue de l'Église • (514) 855-6130

St-Léonard
8420 boul. Lacordaire • (514) 328-8595

T.M.R.
1967 boul. Graham • (514) 734-2967

Verdun
5955 rue Bannantyne • (514) 765-7173

Westmount
4574 rue Sherbrooke O. • (514) 989-5300
www.westlib.org/

There are some independently run institutions in Montréal with books and programs for children.

Fraser-Hickson Institute
4855 av. Kensington • (514) 489-5301
www.FraserHickson.qc.ca

Jewish Public Library
5151 Côte Ste-Catherine • (514) 345-2627
www.jewishpubliclibrary.org

Montréal Children's Library
1200 av. Atwater • (514) 931-2304
www.dsuper.net/~mcl-bjm

Cool Places to Play SWIMMING POOLS

For kids, the best place to spend a hot summer afternoon is at the local pool. Most community pools, whether indoor or outdoor, have swimming lessons for children of all ages. Other aquatic sports are also frequently available. While some municipal pools refuse entry to babies in diapers, others welcome them. Some even host birthday parties. Indoor swimming is offered at the following locations unless otherwise indicated.

ANJOU
ÉCOLE SECONDAIRE ANJOU
(AFTER 4 PM)
8205 RUE FONTENAU
(514) 493-8223

BEACONSFIELD
CENTRE RÉCRÉATIF
1974 LANE CITY
(514) 428-4520

CHÂTEAUGUAY
POLYDIUM
111 BOUL. MAPLE
(450) 698-3120

CÔTE-ST-LUC
(OUTDOOR)
7005 CH. MACKLE
(514) 485-6806

DOLLARD-DES-ORMEAUX
12001 RUE DE SALABERRY
(514) 684-1012

DORVAL
AQUATIC CENTRE
1945 AV. PARKFIELD
(514) 633-4001

HAMPSTEAD
(OUTDOOR)
30 CH. CLEVE
(514) 369-8266

KIRKLAND PARK
(OUTDOOR)
(514) 368-5746

LACHINE
#740 AV. 18
(514) 634-3471 EXT. 301

LA PRAIRIE
575 RUE NOTRE-DAME
(450) 444-6719

LASALLE
AQUADOME
1411 RUE LAPIERRE
(514) 367-6460

LAVAL
FOR THE LOCATIONS AND SCHEDULES OF
LAVAL'S POOLS, CALL (450) 662-4343.

LONGUEUIL
670 RUE DARVEAU
(450) 646-8260

MONTRÉAL
(OUTDOOR POOLS, OPEN BETWEEN JUNE
AND SEPTEMBER)

ALEXIS CARREL
12550 AV. ALEXIS-CARREL
(514) 648-0390

BALDWIN
2330 RUE RACHEL E.
(514) 872-3533

BENNY
6445 AV. MONKLAND
(514) 872-3558

CONFÉDÉRATION
6265 AV. BIERMANS
(514) 872-1125

DES PINS
3975 AV. 42
(514) 642-2940

FRANÇOIS PERRAULT
7601 RUE FRANÇOIS-PERRAULT
(514) 872-1133

GABRIEL LALLEMANT
2350 RUE SAUVÉ E.
(514) 872-1137

G-E CARTIER
4550 RUE STE-ÉMILIE
(514) 872-3539

IGNACE BOURGET
5925 AV. DE MONTMAGNY
(514) 872-1120

ÎLE STE-HÉLÈNE POOL
ÎLE STE-HÉLÈNE
(514) 872-3526

JARRY
205 RUE FAILLON O.
(514) 872-1135

JOSEPH PARÉ
6525 AV. 41
(514) 872-1130

KENT
6262 CH. HUDSON
(514) 872-4697

LE PELICAN
2560 RUE MASSON
(514) 872-3589

L-O TAILLON
9200 RUE NOTRE-DAME E.
(514) 872-1126

MARCELLIN WILSON
1655 RUE DUDEMAINE
(514) 872-1138

PARC PLAGE
ÎLE NOTRE-DAME
(514) 872-4537

RICHELIEU
285 RUE RICHELIEU
(514) 642-2836

ST GEORGES
13000 RUE PRINCE-ALBERT
(514) 640-4320

STE-LUCIE
9093 AV. 16
(514) 872-1134

STE-MARIE
15744 RUE NOTRE DAME E.
(514) 642-4044

SIR WILFRID-LAURIER
5200 RUE DE BRÉBEUF
(514) 872-4050

(INDOOR POOLS)
CENTRE DU PLATEAU
2275 BOUL. ST-JOSEPH E.
(514) 872-6830

CENTRE SPORTIF CÔTE-DES-NEIGES
4880 AV. VAN HORNE
(514) 342-9988

CENTRE SPORTIF PETITE BOURGOGNE
1825 RUE NOTRE-DAME O.
(514) 932-0800

CLAUDE ROBILLARD
1000 AV. ÉMILE JOURNAULT
(514) 872-6905

COLLÈGE DE MAISONNEUVE
2701 RUE NICOLET
(514) 254-7131

ÉDOUARD MONTPETIT
6100 AV. PIERRE-DE COUBERTIN
(514) 872-6171

EMARD
6071 RUE LAURENDEAU
(514) 872-2585

EPIC
5055 RUE ST-ZOTIQUE
(514) 872-6598

GADBOIS
5485 CH. DE LA CÔTE-ST-PAUL
(514) 872-2581

GEORGES VERNOT
8475 AV. 13
(514) 872-5605

HOCHELAGA
1870 RUE DAVIDSON
(514) 872-2105

JOHN-F-KENNEDY
3030 RUE VILLERAY
(514) 872-5608

JOSEPH CHARBONNEAU
8200 RUE ROUSSELOT
(514) 872-3261

LÉVESQUE
4356 RUE BOYER
(514) 872-2823

MORGAN
1875 AV. MORGAN
(514) 872-6657

NOTRE-DAME-DE-GRÂCE
3760 BOUL. DÉCARIE
(514) 872-6285

PATRO LE PRÉVOST
7355 AV. CHRISTOPHE COLUMB
(514) 273-8535

PÈRE MARQUETTE
1600 RUE DE DRUCOURT
(514) 872-4714

POINTE-AUX-TREMBLES
15200 RUE SHERBROOKE E.
(514) 872-6237

QUINTAL
1550 RUE DUFRESNE
(514) 872-2864

RENÉ-GOUPIL
4250 RUE RENÉ-GOUPIL
(514) 872-5632

RIVIÈRE DES PRAIRIES
12515 BOUL. RODOLPHE FORGET
(514) 872-9322

ROSEMONT
6101 AV. 8
(514) 872-6622

ROUSSIN
12125 RUE NOTRE-DAME E.
(514) 645-4519

ST-CHARLES
1055 RUE HIBERNIA
(514) 872-2501

ST-DENIS
7075 RUE ST-HUBERT
(514) 872-4651

ST-HENRI
4055 RUE ST-JACQUES O.
(514) 872-2577

SCHUBERT
3950 RUE ST-LAURENT
(514) 872-2587

SOPHIE-BARAT
10851 AV. ST-CHARLES
(514) 872-1136

VIEUX MONTRÉAL
255 RUE ONTARIO E.
(514) 982-3457

WESTHILL
5945 AV. SOMERLED
(514) 872-6206

YMCA HOCHELAGA-MAISONNEUVE
4567 RUE HOCHELAGA
(514) 255-4651

MONTRÉAL EAST
CENTRE RÉCRÉATIF
ÉDOUARD-RIVET
11111 RUE NOTRE-DAME E.
(514) 640-2737

MONTRÉAL NORTH
RECREATION DEPARTMENT
(514) 328-4160

CALIXA-LAVALLÉE POOL
11345 AV. PELLETIER
(514) 328-4170

HENRI-BOURASSA POOL
12005 AV. LAURIER
(514) 328-4171

MONTRÉAL WEST
(OUTDOOR POOL)
220 AV. BEDBROOK
(514) 489-6472

OUTREMONT
J-F-KENNEDY POOL
860 AV. OUTREMONT
(514) 495-6253

PIERREFONDS
PIERREFONDS HAS NO INDOOR POOLS, BUT RESIDENTS CAN USE THOSE IN POINTE-CLAIRE AND DOLLARD-DES-ORMEAUX.

POINTE-CLAIRE
98 AV. DOUGLAS-SHAND
(514) 630-1202

REPENTIGNY
130 RUE VALMONT
(450) 654-2401

STE-ANNE-DE-BELLEVUE
PUBLIC SWIMMING IS AVAILABLE AT JOHN ABBOTT COLLEGE
(514) 457-2737

ST-HUBERT
CENTRE SPORTIF ROSANNE-LAFLAMME
(450) 445-7791

ST-LAMBERT
325 RUE L'ÉSPÉRANCE
(450) 923-6595

ST-LAURENT
PUBLIC SWIMMING IS AVAILABLE ONLY TO RESIDENTS WHO HAVE PURCHASED A "CARTE DE LOISIRS." FOR MORE INFORMATION, CALL 855-6110 OR GO TO WWW.VILLE.SAINT-LAURENT.QC.CA.

ST-LÉONARD
5115 RUE DES GALETS
(514) 328-8595

T.M.R.
(OUTDOOR)
1000 CH. DUNKIRK
(514) 734-2948

VERDUN
(OUTDOOR)
6500 BOUL. LASALLE
(514) 765-7230

WESTMOUNT
(OUTDOOR)
(BESIDE THE WESTMOUNT ARENA)
4765 RUE STE-CATHERINE O.
(514) 989-5353

Cool Places to Play II
CITY RINKS

I f you like to strap on skates, you're in luck. There's no shortage of skating rinks in the Montréal area. While hockey, figure skating and other organized activities often dominate the ice time, arenas usually set aside several hours each week for public skating. Call your municipal rink for information about its schedule of activities.

ANJOU
CHAUMONT ARENA
8750 AV. CHAUMONT
(514) 493-8256

BEACONSFIELD
BEACONSFIELD ARENA
CENTRE RÉCRÉATIF
1974 LANE CITY
(514) 428-4520

CHÂTEAUGUAY
GUY SCOTT ARENA
75 BOUL. MAPLE
(450) 698-3110

LÉO CRÉPIN ARENA
255 BOUL. BRISEBOIS
(450) 698-3140

CÔTE-ST-LUC
SAMUEL-MOSKOVITCH ARENA
6985 CH. MACKLE
(514) 485-6802

DELSON
DELSON ARENA
50 RUE STE-THÉRÈSE
(450) 632-9352

DOLLARD-DES-ORMEAUX
ARENA 3
12001 RUE DE SALABERRY
(514) 684-1012

DORVAL
DORVAL ARENA
1450 AV. DAWSON
(514) 633-4010

HAMPSTEAD
FOR INFORMATION ABOUT THE SCHEDULES
AND LOCATIONS OF OUTDOOR RINKS CALL
(514) 369-8270.

LACHINE
LACHINE ARENA
1925 RUE ST-ANTOINE
(514) 634-3471 EXT. 301

ST-PIERRE ARENA
183 RUE DES ÉRABLES
(514) 368-5744

LAVAL
FOR THE LOCATIONS OF AND SCHEDULES
OF LAVAL'S RINKS, CALL (450) 662-4343.

LONGUEUIL

JACQUES-CARTIER ARENA
1143 RUE DELORIMIER
(450) 646-8580

OLYMPIA ARENA
2950 RUE DUMONT
(450) 646-8585

MONTRÉAL

AHUNTSIC
10560 RUE ST-HUBERT
(514) 872-6115

BILL DURNAN
4988 RUE VÉZINA
(514) 872-6073

CAMILLIEN HOUDE
1696 RUE MONTCALM
(514) 872-3240

CLÉMENT JETTÉ
8780 AV. DUBUISSON
(514) 872-6708

DOUG HARVEY
4985 AV. WEST HILL
(514) 872-6028

ÉTIENNE DESMARTEAU
3430 RUE DE BELLECHASSE
(514) 872-6578

GEORGES ET SYLVIO MANTHA
5485 CH. DE LA CÔTE-ST-PAUL
(514) 872-2755

HOWIE MORENZ
8650 AV. QUERBES
(514) 872-6672

JEAN ROUGEAU
8000 RUE DE NORMANVILLE
(514) 872-6689

MARCELLIN WILSON
11301 BOUL. DE L'ACADIE
(514) 872-6191

MAURICE-RICHARD
2800 RUE VIAU
(514) 872-6666

MICHEL NORMANDIN
850 AV. ÉMILE JOURNAULT
(514) 872-6913

MONT-ROYAL
4365 RUE CARTIER
(514) 872-4705

PÈRE-MARQUETTE
1605 RUE DE BELLECHASSE
(514) 872-4073

RAYMOND PRÉFONTAINE
3175 RUE DE ROUEN
(514) 872-6621

RENÉ MASSON
9175 BOUL. PERRAS
(514) 872-6266

RODRIGUE GILBERT
1515 BOUL. DU TRICENTENAIRE
(514) 872-6104

ST-CHARLES
1055 RUE HIBERNIA
(514) 872-3300

ST-DONAT
6750 RUE DE MARSEILLE
(514) 872-6764

ST-LOUIS
5633 RUE ST-DOMINIQUE
(514) 872-2062

ST-MICHEL
3440 RUE JARRY E.
(514) 872-3491

YMCA HOCHELAGA-MAISONNEUVE
4567 RUE HOCHELAGA
(514) 255-4651

MONTRÉAL EAST

CENTRE RÉCRÉATIF ÉDOUARD-RIVET
11111 RUE NOTRE-DAME E.
(514) 640-2737

MONTRÉAL NORTH

FLEURY ARENA
3700 RUE FLEURY E.
(514) 328-4161

HENRI-BOURASSA ARENA
12000 BOUL. ROLLAND
(514) 328-4162

MONTRÉAL NORTH ARENA
11212 AV. GARON
(514) 328-4163

MONTRÉAL WEST

220 AV. BEDBROOK
(514) 489-8448

OUTREMONT
999 AV. MCEACHRAN
(514) 495-6231

PIERREFONDS
13777 BOUL. PIERREFONDS
(514) 624-1124

POINTE-CLAIRE
96 AV. DOUGLAS-SHAND
(514) 630-1211

REPENTIGNY
80 BOUL. BRIEN
(450) 581-7060

ST-CONSTANT
260 RTE. 132
(450) 635-8414

ST-LAMBERT
616 AV. OAK
(450) 923-6609

ST-LAURENT
CENTRE SPORTIF RAYMOND-
BOURQUE
2345 BOUL. THIMENS
(514) 956-2580

ST-LÉONARD
ST-LÉONARD ARENA
5300 BOUL. ROBERT
(514) 328-8499

HÉBERT ARENA
7755 RUE COLBERT
(514) 328-8495

T.M.R.
1050 CH. DUNKIRK
(514) 734-2928

WESTMOUNT
4765 RUE STE-CATHERINE O.
(514) 989-5353

CHAPTER 5

PLACES TO PLAY

Introduction

I f it were left up to kids, they'd play all day long. Fortunately for them the Montréal area is full of parks, amusement centres and other affordable destinations where children's fun is the number-one priority all year long. Delight in a recreation of Alice's Wonderland. Be a guest at the biggest winter party in Montréal, La Fête des Neiges. Fly through the air on a trapeze. Visit the site of the old Expo '67—it's certainly changed over the years. Try your hand at indoor rock climbing. You'll get hooked! This chapter will also tell you where to find the best tobogganing runs and swimming beaches.

For parents looking to do something extra-special for their child's birthday this year, read on to discover which sites have accommodations for children's parties. Then make your plans. Whole days of fun await you.

Zipping Down
A WATERSLIDE

I s there any better way to spend a hot, sunny day than slipping down a waterslide into a refreshing pool of water? Luckily for Montréalers there are several water parks within an hour or so from the city.

Each site offers visitors such attractions as giant slides, swimming pools, tarzan swings, leisure pools, tube rafting and pedal boats. Some parks even have pools for younger children. Visiting a waterslide park will bring out the kid in everyone.

PARK AQUATIQUE BROMONT
(450) 866-4270
HWY. 10 E. TOWARDS SHERBROOKE, EXIT 78.
ABOUT 45 MINUTES FROM DOWNTOWN.

PARC AQUATIQUE MONT ST-SAUVEUR
(450) 227-4671
WWW.MONTSAINTSAUVEUR.COM
HWY. 15 N., EXIT 58.
ABOUT 50 MINUTES FROM DOWNTOWN.

SUPER AQUA CLUB, POINTE-CALUMET (NEAR OKA)
(450) 473-1013
HWY. 640 W., EXIT 2.
ABOUT 30 MINUTES FROM DOWNTOWN.

SUPER SPLASH, STE-ADÈLE
(450) 229-2909
HWY. 15 N., EXIT 67.
ABOUT ONE HOUR FROM DOWNTOWN.

☞ **SEASONS AND TIMES**
➤ Summer: Mid-June—Labour Day, daily, 10 am—7 pm.

☞ **COST**
➤ Adults $20, children $10.
(Prices may vary between sites.)

☞ **SIMILAR ATTRACTIONS**
➤ **Cascades d'Eau Glissades**
222 ch. des Cascadelles
Piedmont
(450) 227-3353.

➤ **Aqua Parc Ski Bromont**
150 Champlain
Bromont
(450) 534-2200 or 1-888-866-4270
www.skibromont.com

➤ **Granby Zoo and Park Safari**
also have water parks (see Chapter 8, pages 151 and 160 respectively).

Whooping it Up at LA RONDE

PARC DES ÎLES
ÎLE STE-HÉLÈNE
MONTRÉAL
(514) 872-6222 OR **1-800-797-4537**
WWW.PDI-MONTREAL.COM

Two words describe Québec's largest amusement park; unadulterated fun. From Le Monstre—the tallest wooden twin-track roller coaster in the world—to the children's carousels, La Ronde has over 30 rides to offer thrill seekers from the timid to the boldest. For an evening treat, stay late and watch the fireworks competition (held in June and July each year).

Small children who do not meet the minimum height and weight requirements for the bigger rides will enjoy La Petite Ronde, a section of the park with rides and activities designed just for them. Look for the children's theatre, Nintendo™ games and the balloon ride, which are also found here.

☞ **SEASONS AND TIMES**
➤ Mid-May—June 1, Sat—Sun, 11 am—11 pm.
June 1—Sept 1, daily from 11 am.
Closing hours vary on certain dates, call for information.
The season is sometimes extended to mid-September, weekends only.

☞ **COST**
➤ Adults $29, children (3 to 11) $15.50, under 3 free.

☞ **GETTING THERE**
➤ By car, follow the Jacques Cartier Bridge, staying in the right lane. Take the Île Ste-Hélène exit and follow the signs. Pay parking on site. About ten minutes from Montréal.
➤ By public transit, take the metro (yellow line) to the Île-Ste-Hélène station, then board the 167 bus.
➤ By bicycle, follow the Lachine Canal bike path and take the Cité du Havre turnoff. Ride across the Concorde Bridge to Île Ste-Hélène. Turn left and pedal to the north-eastern tip of the island.

La Ronde also has swimming pools and there's a children's playground and a shaded picnicking site nearby. Keep your ticket stub for readmission.

☞ **NEARBY**
➤ Biosphere, Stewart Museum, Plages des Îles.

☞ **COMMENT**
➤ Bring hats and sunscreen—shade is hard to find. Plan a half-day visit.

Indoor
ROCK CLIMBING

Most kids have an inborn love of climbing. Why not satisfy their desire to get higher with a visit to an indoor centre that has rock climbing facilities? You'll find qualified staff ready to instruct your children in proper techniques on routes that have been designed to accommodate climbers of every ability. Safety equipment is provided and supervisory personnel are always on hand. Children as young as five are welcome. Climbing is an excellent exercise that builds body strength and the ability to concentrate—so adults should give it a try too!

Schedules can vary, so please call ahead.

HORIZON ROC
2350 RUE DICKSON
MONTRÉAL
(514) 899-5000 OR (514) 899-8561
WWW.CAM.ORG/~ORG

Canada's largest indoor climbing centre also features tarzan swings, games, youth clubs and more. One section is just for children under six.

With suitable supervision, kids as young as three are welcome. The centre requires everyone to take a three-hour introductory lesson to rock climbing. Outdoor summer courses are also offered.

☞ Year-round: Daily, 10 am—3 pm, 5 pm—11 pm.

☞ $11 per day or $28.75 per month.

ESCALADE ACTION DIRECTE
4377 BOUL. ST-ELZÉAR O.
LAVAL
(450) 688-0515

☞ Year-round: Mon—Fri, 5 pm—11 pm; Sat, 9 am—10 pm; Sun, 9 am—9 pm.

☞ $11.50 per child per hour, which includes a trained spotter. Parents can take a course so they can supervise their own children. Mobile climbing towers are available for rental.

ALLEZ-UP
1339 RUE SHEARER
MONTRÉAL
(514) 989-9656

Offers indoor rock climbing as well as summer climbing excursions to the Laurentians. Reservations required.

☞ Year-round: Mon—Tue, 4 pm—11 pm; Wed, 2 pm—11 pm; Thu—Fri, noon—11 pm; weekends, 9 am—9 pm.

☞ $15 an hour.

Celebrating Winter at
FÊTE DES NEIGES

Parc des Îles
Île Ste-Hélène
Montréal
http://pdi-montreal.com
(514) 872-4537

For two weeks every winter, Île Ste-Hélène becomes the site of a gigantic, outdoor festival. It's the Fête des Neiges, a crazy winter party designed with kids in mind. Your family can easily spend a full day seeing ice sculptures and snow castles, playing with Disney characters and riding on dog sleds and horse-drawn sleighs. Your kids can race around the labyrinth, explore an enchanted forest or even visit a miniature farm. Face painting is offered or they can go snow tubing, or try curling and ice-skating on the Olympic Basin.

The festival is a popular event and well attended on weekends. Motorists may have to park more than a kilometre from the site, so bring a sled to pull your kids and gear and dress warmly. It gets very windy on the island.

☞ **SEASONS AND TIMES**
➤ Late Jan—mid-Feb: Mon—Fri, 9:30 am—3:30 pm; Sat—Sun, 10 am—5 pm.

☞ **COST**
➤ Free to enter. $3 to $10 per person for most activities or you can buy a $5 pass ($4 at some McDonald's) that gives you reduced rates on some activities.

☞ **GETTING THERE**
➤ By car, access Île Ste-Hélène via the Jacques Cartier Bridge. Follow the signs for La Ronde. Parking on site for $8. About 10 minutes from downtown.
➤ By public transit, take the metro (yellow line) to the Île-Ste-Hélène metro station.

☞ **NEARBY**
➤ Stewart Museum, Biosphere.

Running Wild in
INDOOR GYMS

D o your children have energy to burn? Take them to an indoor adventure gym where slides, climbing nets, tunnels and pedal cars are made-to-measure for kids. If that's not adventurous enough, what about trying the trapeze?

Even though staff are on hand, children must be accompanied by a supervising adult and wear socks at all times. Most indoor gyms rent rooms for special occasions such as birthday parties. Some centres have reduced hours in the summer.

BANANAZOO
900 BOUL. CURÉ-LABELLE
LAVAL
(450) 688-8880 OR 1-877-752-4747
WWW.RECREATHEQUE.COM

☞ Year-round: Daily, 10 am—7 pm.

☞ Adults free, children's day pass Mon—Fri $6.15; Sat—Sun $7.85.

BOOMERANG
7852 BOUL. CHAMPLAIN
LASALLE
(514) 365-9830

☞ Year-round: Sun—Thu, 10 am—5 pm; Fri—Sat, 10 am—7 pm.

☞ Children's day pass Mon—Fri $5.95; Sat—Sun $7.95; kids under 2 Mon—Fri $4.95; Sat—Sun $6.95.

EXPLORATION
5000 BOUL. TASCHEREAU E.
BROSSARD
(450) 671-1212

☞ Year-round: Sat—Sun, 10 am—5 pm.

☞ $7 per child.

JUNGLE ADVENTURE
GALERIES DE LAVAL
1595 BOUL. LE CORBUSIER
LAVAL
(450) 681-2144

☞ Year-round: Mon—Thu, 10 am—6 pm; Fri—Sun, 10 am—8 pm.

☞ Children (2 to 13) Mon—Fri $5.95; Sat, Sun, and holidays
$7.95. Memberships and group rates available.

KIDNASIUM
6263 AV. SOMERLED
MONTRÉAL
(514) 482-8659

Kidnasium's primary focus is the large gymnasium where children up to seven years of age can take non-competitive gym courses. There is also a smaller playroom available for day use. Bring your own lunch. There is a no peanuts policy.

☞ Year-round: Mon—Thu, 9 am—3:30 pm.

☞ $7 per child.

La Cache a l'Eau
1235 RUE AMPÈRE
BOUCHERVILLE
(450) 641-0312

☞ Year-round: Mon—Thu, 10 am—6 pm, Fri—Sun, 10 am—7 pm.

☞ Mon—Fri $5.95, Sat—Sun $7.95.

L'orange bleu
LE GARDEUR
460 BOUL. LACOMBE
(450) 657-8484

☞ Year-round: Mon—Fri, 10 am—6 pm; Sat—Sun, 10 am—8 pm.

☞ Mon—Fri $5.95; Sat—Sun $7.40.

Trapezium
2350 RUE DICKSON
MONTRÉAL
(514) 251-0615
HTTP://TRAPEZIUM.QC.CA

Children seven and up can learn the ropes on the flying trapeze. Circus theme birthdays can be arranged.

☞ Adults, Mon—Fri, 7 pm; children, Sat—Sun, 1 pm.
Trials: Sat—Sun, 1 pm.

☞ Prices start at $7 for a trial.

Team Sports at FORT ANGRIGNON

RUE LACROIX AND BOUL. DES TRINITAIRES
(LACROIX ST. AND DES TRINITAIRES BLVD)
MONTRÉAL
(514) 872-3816

This indoor site provides a variety of adventure packages that include such activities as crawling through labyrinths, scaling walls and running obstacle courses. Depending on the season, water sports or inner tube sledding may be on the menu.

Aspiring adventurers (ages six and up) need to form teams of 8 to 12 people before making reservations for a weekend course which takes about two-and-a-half hours to complete. Participants are advised to bring a lunch although a snack bar is available.

Weekdays are set aside for 5 to 17 year-olds (minimum group size 25). Reservations are necessary. Both half-day and full day packages are available.

☞ **SEASONS AND TIMES**
➼ Winter: Early Dec—late Mar. Summer: May—late Oct. Visits by appointment only.

☞ **COST**
➼ Adults $9, children (6 to 17) $7.50. School group prices start at $5 per person for a half day. Discounts available for Montréal residents.

☞ **GETTING THERE**
➼ By car, take Hwy. 15 south to Exit 62 and drive west on de la Vérendrye Blvd. At des Trinitaires Blvd., turn right and follow the signs for metro parking. The fort is across the parking lot from the Angrignon metro station. It's a 15–minute drive. Pay parking on weekdays, free on weekends.
➼ By public transit, take the metro (green line) to the Angrignon station and walk across the parking lot. It's about a five-minute walk.
➼ By bicycle, exit Lachine Canal bike path just west of Atwater Market on Angers St. bike path. This leads onto the Aqueduct bike path (beside Champlain Blvd.), which leads to Angrignon Park. The Fort is at the far end of the park.

☞ **NEARBY**
➼ Angrignon Farm, Aquadome.

☞ **COMMENT**
➼ Plan a half-day visit. Sport clothes and swimsuits (in season) must be worn.

Birthday parties with animation and supervision can also be arranged.

Puttering Around at MINIGOLF

Thirty minutes and a good sense of humour are all it takes to play 18 holes of minigolf. While the principle is the same as regular golf—sink the ball in the hole using the fewest strokes—this scaled-down version puts obstacles between you and your target. The better the course, the better the obstacles, which may include tunnels, bridges, water, windmills and silhouettes

> ☞ **SEASONS AND TIMES**
> ➤ May—Oct, daily during mid-summer, weekends only at the start and end of the season. 10 am—dusk.
>
> ☞ **COST**
> ➤ Varies, but generally: Adults $6, children $4.

of popular cartoon characters. Most kids love the challenge, but some will be frustrated by a game that looks easier than it is. Balls, putters and scorecards are supplied, though it's up to you whether you keep score or not. After playing a round, head to the "club-house" for an ice cream or other refreshment. Some minigolf courses host children's birthday parties.

MINI-PUTT JEAN-TALON
4400 RUE JEAN-TALON E., ST-LÉONARD • (514) 727-5143

MINI-PUTT ET LANCES BALLES LASALLE
7077 BOUL. NEWMAN, LASALLE • (514) 595-5778

Mini-Putt Versailles
7220 RUE SHERBROOKE E. • (514) 252-7372

Mini-Putt Vimont 36 Trous
1950 BOUL. LAURENTIEN, VIMONT • (450) 629-9731

Récréathèque (indoor, year-round site)
990 BOUL. CURÉ-LABELLE, LAVAL • (450) 688-8880

Golf-Cité
100 CH. DE LA POINTE N, ÎLE DES SOEURS • (514) 769-7770

Mini-Golf Don Quichotte
106 BOUL. DON QUICHOTTE, ÎLE PERROT • (514) 453-8440

Take a Break at McDONALD'S™ PLAYLANDS

D id you know your kids are welcome at McDonald's™ play areas even if you don't buy a meal from the restaurant? A godsend during bad weather, these indoor parks feature tunnel slides, carousels and rooms filled with plastic balls. Though the layout varies from outlet to outlet, several tables in each restaurant juxtapose the glassed-in area, permitting parents to quietly sip a cup of coffee while watching the kids. Should you decide to purchase food, children can

---

☞ **Seasons and Times**
→ Year-round: Daily, 7 am–10 pm.
(May vary according to restaurant.)

☞ **Cost**
→ Free (meals extra).

order a kid-size meal that comes with a toy. Disposable bibs and highchairs are available and the place mats can be coloured, so bring crayons. Birthday parties can be arranged.

On Montréal Island
7270 RUE ST-JACQUES, MONTRÉAL
4928 BOUL. DES SOURCES, DORVAL
4900 RUE JEAN-TALON E., MONTRÉAL
12090 RUE SHERBROOKE EST, POINTE-AUX-TREMBLES
10333 BOUL. PIE-IX, MONTRÉAL NORTH
7275 BOUL. ST-LAURENT, MONTRÉAL
5350 AV. DU PARC, MONTRÉAL

South Shore, Montérégie, Les Cantons de l'Est (Eastern Townships)
661 BOUL. DU SÉMINAIRE, ST-JEAN-SUR-RICHELIEU
870 RUE PRINCIPALE, GRANBY
7450 BOUL. TASCHEREAU, BROSSARD
3279 BOUL. TASCHEREAU, GREENFIELD PARK

Laval, North Shore
1400 BOUL. MOODY, TERREBONNE
185 RUE NOTRE-DAME, REPENTIGNY
2005 BOUL. ST-MARTIN O., LAVAL
797 BOUL. CURÉ-LABELLE, BLAINVILLE

Sandy
SWIMMING BEACHES

Nothing beats the summer heat like a swim at the beach. Luckily for Montréalers, there are scores of sandy beaches nearby just perfect for families to visit, including one that's minutes from downtown. Not all of these sites offer supervised swimming and some have modest user fees. Changing facilities, toilets and concession stands are usually found nearby. Watercraft can be rented at some locations.

PLAGE DES ÎLES
PARC DES ÎLES, ÎLE NOTRE DAME
MONTRÉAL
(514) 872-6093

ST-TIMOTHÉE REGIONAL PARK
(NEAR VALLEYFIELD)
(450) 377-1117
(AUTOBUS CITSO FROM METRO ANGRIGNON – 450-698-3030)

CAP ST-JACQUES
20099 BOUL. GOUIN O.
PIERREFONDS
(514) 280-6778

ÎLE-BIZARD REGIONAL PARK
2115 CH. BORD-DU-LAC
ÎLE-BIZARD
(514) 280-8517

OKA PARK
(NEAR ST-EUSTACHE)
HWY. 640 O.
(450) 479-8337 OR 1-888-727-2652 • WWW.SEPAQ.COM

ST-ZOTIQUE
(NEAR VALLEYFIELD)
(450) 267-9335

STE-CATHERINE
(NEAR MERCIER BRIDGE)
(450) 632-0590 OR 635-3011

PLATTSBURGH CITY BEACH
BEACH ROAD, PLATTSBURGH, NY
(518) 563-4431

Great
TOBOGGANING HILLS

Everyone has stories about "the best" toboggan-ing hill. That's because everyone loves tobog-ganing, even those of us who have forgotten what it feels like to career down a snowy slope on a piece of wood or plastic that threatens to go out of control at any moment. The following is a listing of popular tobogganing runs in the Montréal area. Take your kids, and this time don't just stand at the top of the hill . . . go for a ride yourself, one more time.

MURRAY HILL PARK
AV. WESTMOUNT AND AV. MURRAY HILL
WESTMOUNT
(514) 989-5353

BEAVER LAKE (MOUNT ROYAL PARK)
VOIE CAMILLIEN-HOUDE
MONTRÉAL
(514) 872-6559
WWW.VILLE.MONTREAL.QC.CA/PARCS

CENTENNIAL PARK
CH. MACKLE AND AV. STEPHEN-LEACOCK
CÔTE ST-LUC
(514) 485-6806

POINTE-AUX-PRAIRIES REGIONAL PARK
12980 BOUL. GOUIN E.
MONTRÉAL
(514) 280-6691

OKA PARK
2200 PAUL SAUVÉ
OKA
(450) 479-8337

MONT ST-HILAIRE CENTRE FOR NATURE CONSERVATION
422 CH. DES MOULINS
ST-HILAIRE
(450) 467-1755

LAVAL NATURE CENTRE
901 AV. DU PARC
LAVAL
(450) 662-4942

LONGUEUIL REGIONAL PARK
1895 RUE ADONCOUR
LONGUEUIL
(450) 646-8269

RIVIÈRE DU NORD REGIONAL PARK
1051 BOUL. INTERNATIONAL
ST-JÉRÔME
(450) 431-1676

CENTRE ÉCOLOGIQUE FERNAND SÉGUIN
RTE. 132 (BEHIND L.P. PARÉ POLYVALENT SCHOOL)
CHÂTEAUGUAY
(450) 698-3123 OR 698-3104

Don't have a toboggan? Why not try snow-tubing, where you ride down specially designed slides in a rented inner tube or raft (helmets are recommended for younger children). Here are some snow tubing sites in the Montréal area. Many have lifts, so you don't have to face the long trudge back to the top of the hill.

LES GLISSADES DU PAYS EN HAUT
440 CH. AVILA
PIEDMONT
(450) 224-4014 OR 1-800-668-7951

MONT AVILA PARC DES NEIGES
HWY. 15 N.
MONT AVILA
(450) 227-4671

SUPER GLISSADES DE ST-JEAN-DE-MATHA
545 CH. PAIN-DE-SUCRE
ST-JEAN-DE-MATHA
(450) 886-9321

Visiting Wonderland at AU PAYS DES MERVEILLES

3595 CH. DE LA SAVANE (SAVANE ROAD)
STE-ADÈLE
(450) 229-3141

Amusement parks with walking life-size story-book characters are always a hit with children, and Au Pays des Merveilles (Wonderland) is no exception. Your kids will delight in meeting Alice and her friends at this park, which is based on the adventures of Lewis Carroll's Alice in Wonderland.

Kids will also discover a playground, a tricycle race track, a minigolf course and even a haunted house, which are all situated along the asphalt paths that lead through this hilly, wooded site.

They'll love finding their way out of the castle maze and playing in the fairy-tale houses. If they have any energy left, your kids can splash in the wading pool, or bounce on the giant, rubber stage.

☞ **SEASONS AND TIMES**
→ Spring: Late May—June 24, Sat—Sun, 10 am—6 pm.
Summer: June 24—late Aug, daily, 10 am—6 pm.
Fall: Sept, Sat—Sun, 10 am—6 pm, weather permitting.
Entrance closes at 4:30 pm.

☞ **COST**
→ General admission: $8.25.

☞ **GETTING THERE**
→ By car, take Hwy. 15 N. to Exit 72, then follow the signs. About one hour from downtown. Free parking on site.

☞ **COMMENT**
→ Plan a half-day visit.

Other Places to Play

Laser Quest

1226 RUE ST-CATHERINE O.
MONTRÉAL
(514) 393-3000
PEEL METRO

Explore the darkened labyrinth, using your laser gun to shoot the opposing team before they can shoot you. Each game lasts 20 minutes. Birthday parties available.

☞ Year-round: Tue—Thu, 6 pm—10 pm; Fri, 5 pm—midnight; Sat, 10 am—midnight; Sun, 1 pm—10 pm. Mondays reserved for groups. Reservations recommended on weekends.

☞ $7 per person per game. Groups of ten or more $6 per person.

Laser Dome

6900 BOUL. DÉCARIE
MONTRÉAL
(514) 344-3663
NAMUR METRO

Accumulate team points by deactivating the Omega base as you venture through the five levels of this simulated space station. Games last 30 minutes and are available to children six and older. Reservations recommended. Birthday packages available.

☞ Year-round: Mon—Thu, 5 pm—9 pm; Fri, 5 pm—midnight; Sat, 10 am—midnight; Sun, 10 am—10 pm.

☞ $11.50 per person for a 30 minute session, $19.50 for a 60 minute session. $42 for a family of four, each additional child $8.

Dark Zone
1545 BOUL. LE CORBUSIER
LAVAL
(450) 978-9922

W ander through the corridors, laser at the ready. Test your reflexes against your friends. A game lasts about 15 minutes.

☞ Year-round: Mon—Fri, 4 pm—11 pm (Fri to midnight); Sat, 10 am—midnight; Sun, 10 am—10 pm.

☞ $6.89 per person per game. Mon $19.95 all night; Tue first game regular price, subsequent games $2 each.

I n-line skating all year long for families.

Paladium de Brossard
9525 BOUL. TASCHEREAU
BROSSARD
(450) 659-2966

Paladium de Longueuil
475 BOUL. ROLAND-THERRIEN
LONGUEUIL
(450) 646-9995

☞ Sun, noon—4 pm.

☞ $5.75 per person. Skate rentals available for $3.

Récréathèque
900 BOUL. LABELLE
CHOMEDEY, LAVAL
(450) 688-8880

B esides the Bananazoo indoor adventure gym (page 100), Récréathèque offers bowling, mini-golf, in-line skating, Laser Adventure, a video arcade and more! Birthday parties are available.

☞ Year-round: Daily. Scheduling and pricing vary with the activity. Call Récréathèque for more details.

CHAPTER 6

PLACES TO LEARN

Introduction

Part of the joy of parenting is satisfying your children's endless curiosity about the world around them. There are many sites in the Montréal area that will help you do this in a fun way. This chapter includes locations where kids can meet an electric eel, learn where honey comes from, visit a hydro-electric dam, spy on a falcon's nest and blast into space. Shhh! Just don't tell them these outings are educational.

Exploring Space at THE COSMODOME

2150 AUTOROUTE LAURENTIEN (LAURENTIAN AUTOROUTE)
LAVAL
(450) 978-3600 • 1-800-565-CAMP
WWW.COSMODOME.ORG

Even if there are no space cadet wanna-be's in your family, a visit to the Cosmodome will still make a fun afternoon outing for your children.

This science centre has hands-on displays and interactive exhibits with eye-popping graphics and great sound effects to teach visitors about aerospace technology and space exploration. The gift shop has space-themed merchandise for sale, including toy rockets that actually blast off.

Most of the exhibits are geared toward children aged 12 and up, but younger kids will certainly find some of the displays interesting too. They can watch the multi-media show or play among replica rockets and spaceships. Kids can even explore the shuttle Endeavor and pretend they're astronauts.

☞ SEASONS AND TIMES

→ Summer: June 24–Sept 1, daily, 10 am–6 pm.
Winter: Sept 2–June 23, Tue–Sun, 10 am–6 pm.

☞ COST

→ Adults $8.75, students (6 to 22) $5.50, under 6 free, families $23.

☞ GETTING THERE

→ By car, take Hwy. 15 N. to Exit 9 (St. Martin Blvd. W.) and follow the signs. You can't miss the red and white replica of the rocket outside. Free parking on site. About 30 minutes from downtown.

→ By public transit, take the metro (orange line) to the Henri-Bourassa station, then board the STL 60 bus. Ask the driver where to get off. It's a short walk to the Cosmodome from the bus stop.

☞ COMMENT

→ Plan a 1-hour visit.

If your children want to learn more about space, consider enrolling them in the Cosmodome's space camp. Call 1-800-565-2267 for more information. School visits can be arranged by calling 978-3615.

Catching the Science Bug at
THE ARMAND FRAPPIER MUSEUM

531 BOUL. DES PRAIRIES (DES PRAIRIES BLVD.)
LAVAL
(450) 686-5641
WWW.MUSEE-AFRAPPIER.QC.CA

A rmand Frappier was a Québec-born microbiologist who was an expert on viruses and epidemics. You can learn about the man, his accomplishments and about microbiology at this museum.

Bilingual guides will lead you through the site, or you can explore it on your own at a leisurely pace. You'll find displays about Frappier's pioneering work, which included developing the first vaccination program for tuberculosis in North America and freeze-dried blood for wounded soldiers in World War II. There are microscopes with prepared slides for studying bacteria,

☞ **SEASONS AND TIMES**
➤ Summer: July—Aug, daily, 10 am—5 pm.
Winter: Sept—June, Mon—Fri, 10 am—5 pm.

☞ **COST**
➤ Adults $5, children $2.50, under 5 free.

yeast, paper and other specimens. Explanatory panels (in French only) will tell you about each exhibit.

The museum is designed for students with an elementary knowledge of biology, but a modified tour for kids as young as four is offered. Visitors are given age-appropriate exercises with questions about what they see in the displays. These may involve drawing the three types of microbes or recalling the favourite hobbies of Frappier. A day camp is offered for budding biologists aged 10 to 15 years.

☞ **GETTING THERE**

➤ By car, take Hwy. 15 N. and cross the bridge to Laval. Immediately after the bridge, take Exit 7 and follow signs for boul. des Prairies. Turn east onto des Prairies; you'll see the museum shortly after you cross under the highway. Free parking on site. About 20 minutes from downtown.

➤ By public transit, take the metro (orange line) to the Henri-Bourassa station, then board STL bus 20. Ask the driver where to get off.

☞ **COMMENT**

➤ Only the first floor is wheelchair-accessible. Plan a 1-hour visit.

After your visit, why not stroll through the extensive grassy grounds down to the des Prairies river. If it's a nice day bring a lunch; there are tables where you can enjoy a picnic.

Visiting the Beehives at
INTERMIEL

10291 RANG DE LA FRESNIÈRE (FRESNIÈRE ROW)
ST-BENOÎT-DE-MIRABEL
(450) 258-2713
WWW.CLOXT.COM/INTERMIEL/

☞ **SEASONS AND TIMES**
➥ Year-round: Daily, 10 am—4 pm.
Beehive opens at 11 am.

☞ **COST**
➥ Adults $3, children $1, under 3
free. Group rates are available.

☞ **GETTING THERE**
➥ By car, take Highway 15 N. to
Highway 640 W. and drive toward
Oka. Exit at Ste-Marthe (Exit 8) and
follow the signs to Intermiel. It's
about a 15-kilometre drive from the
640. Free parking on site. About 50
minutes from downtown.

☞ **NEARBY**
➥ Exotarium and apple orchards.

☞ **COMMENT**
➥ Plan a 2-hour visit.

☞ **SIMILAR ATTRACTION**
➥ **Meillerie Deschamps**, 5510 25th
Ave., St-Eustache, (450) 473-5470.

Intermiel offers kids a wonderful opportunity to learn all about bees and how honey is made. This working apiary has approximately 1500 beehives (making it the largest in Québec) and provides guided tours of its operations in English and French. During the tour, you will learn how bees transform nectar into honey and you'll get to view beekeepers tending the hives and gathering the honey. You'll even get to taste some. Later, from the safety of a glassed-in veranda, you can watch as a beekeeper opens a hive to let you peek inside.

The Discovery Room has games, puzzles and interactive displays, including a giant model of a bee and two computers with bee-themed software that children can use. They can also watch a video about the farm's operations. Visiting groups are entertained with dancing, miming and a puppet show.

There is a playground and petting zoo on-site. Bring your bikes when you visit as bicycling is very good along flat, rural la Fresnière Row. There are many pick-your-own apple orchards in the vicinity.

Bulls and Birds
THE MONTRÉAL STOCK EXCHANGE
(and the Peregrine Falcon Information Centre)

800 PLACE VICTORIA
MONTRÉAL
(514) 871-3582 OR **1-800-361-5353** (STOCK EXCHANGE)
WWW.BDM.ORG (STOCK EXCHANGE)
WWW.DEEV.COM/FALCONS/ (FALCON INFORMATION CENTRE)

For an outing that's different, take the kids to the Montréal Stock Exchange. From the Visitor's Gallery they can watch frenzied traders rushing around the trading floor. In the Visitor's Centre nearby, they'll find interactive displays, multimedia presentations and even an interactive game. While the exhibits are designed for those with stock market savvy, children will still enjoy pushing the buttons and making the lights go on. Animators, who work at the centre, will adapt their presentation to suit even the youngest audiences. Kids love the part about the

☞ **SEASONS AND TIMES**
➤ Stock Exchange: Year-round,
Mon—Fri, 8:30 am—4:30 pm.
Groups of 15 or more should make
reservations.
Falcon Centre: Seasonal, Mon—Fri,
9:30 am—4 pm.

☞ **COST**
➤ Free. Donations accepted at the
Falcon Centre.

☞ **GETTING THERE**
➤ By car, take Beaver Hall Hill south
from René-Lévesque Blvd. to St.
Jacques St. and turn east. The Stock
Exchange building is on the north
side. Limited street parking nearby.
➤ By public transit, take the metro
(orange line) to the Square-Victoria
station, exit via St. Jacques and walk
west for about five minutes.

☞ **COMMENT**
➤Plan a 45-minute visit.

traders' secret sign language. A hand-out that explains the sign system is available.

Save time for the Peregrine Falcon Information Centre in the lobby of the Stock Exchange building. It has displays and brochures and there is a high definition television that shows a peregrine nest (usually occupied from early summer to August) on the 32nd floor of the building. A biologist will tell you all about peregrine falcons and their efforts to recover from near extinction in the 1960s. Today, about a dozen nesting pairs live in Québec. To survive, the birds have had to adapt to new environments such as downtown skyscrapers. The centre is co-sponsored by the Avian Research Centre at Macdonald Campus and the law firm of Martineau Walker.

Learning How Cheese is Made at
FROMAGERIE MIRABEL
(Mirabel Cheese Dairy)

150 BOUL. LACHAPELLE (LACHAPELLE BLVD.)
ST-ANTOINE
(450) 438-5822

A re your rug rats cheese lovers? Then here's their chance to see how it's made. At the Fromagerie Mirabel you can watch the entire cheese-making process unfold before you, from the raw milk being delivered through to the packaging of the final product.

The dairy makes over 150 varieties of cheese, but cheddar is the bread and butter of the operation. If your visit happens to fall outside of regular tour hours, you can peek through the windows at the back of the plant where photos depicting every stage of cheese making are displayed on the wall inside the dairy.

The on-site gift shop sells every type of . . . you guessed it, cheese. It also houses a bakery and an eating area. Bon appétit!

☞ **SEASONS AND TIMES**
→ Year-round: Mon—Fri, 9 am—9 pm; Sat—Sun, 10 am—6 pm. Guided tours: Mon—Fri, 2 pm.

☞ **COST**
→ Free.

☞ **GETTING THERE**
→ By car, take Hwy. 15 N. to Exit 39 in St. Antoine, just north of Mirabel Airport, and follow the signs. Free parking on site. About 45 minutes from downtown.

☞ **COMMENT**
→ Plan a 45-minute visit.

☞ **SIMILAR ATTRACTION**
→ **Fromagerie du vieux St-François,** Laval, (450) 666-6610.

Hearing his Master's Voice at MUSÉE DES ONDES ÉMILE BERLINER *(The Sound Museum)*

1050 RUE LACASSE (LACASSE ST.)
MONTRÉAL
(514) 932-9663
WWW.CONTACT.NET/BERLINER/

D id you know that the gramophone was invented in Montréal by Émile Berliner? He is also considered by many to have invented records. You'll learn more about Berliner, a contemporary and rival of Thomas Edison, at this museum that's devoted to sound.

Housed in Berliner's original RCA factory (built in 1908), the museum has a wide-ranging collection, which includes old-time crystal and World War II military radios, early televisions and dictating machines.

☞ **SEASONS AND TIMES**
➤ Year-round: Fri—Sun, 2 pm—5 pm.

☞ **COST**
➤ Adults $3, children under 14 free.

A hand-cranked record player plays 1920s tunes and some of Elvis's first recordings, pressed on site, can be viewed.

Bilingual plaques will tell you about the artifacts and friendly museum volunteers offer tours. Because of the narrative nature of the displays, this museum is best suited for older children.

☞ **GETTING THERE**

➤ By car, take Peel St. south to St. Antoine St. and turn west. Turn north onto Ste-Marguerite St. and go west on Richelieu St. for one block. Free parking on site and on the street. About 10 minutes from downtown.

➤ By public transit, take the metro (orange line) to the Place St. Henri station and walk west for four short blocks.

☞ **NEARBY**

➤ Minutes away on foot at the corner of St. Jacques St. and St. Antoine is a statue of Louis Cyr, a Québec strong man of the late 1800s. Kids are invariably impressed at the girth of the statue's arms and legs.

☞ **COMMENT**

➤No wheelchair access. Plan a 30-minute visit.

Getting a Charge Out of
THE ÉLECTRIUM

2001 MICHAEL FARADAY
STE-JULIE
(450) 652-8977 OR 1-800-267-4558
WWW.HYDROQUEBEC.COM/VISITEZ/MONTEREGIE/ELECTRIUM.HTML

I f talk about volts and watts leaves you in the dark, a visit to the Électrium should be illuminating. Hydro-Québec's Electricity and Magnetic Field Interpretation Centre has loads of interactive displays to teach visitors about electricity.

Friendly bilingual staff will guide you through magnetic fields, help you to understand lightning and explain the physics of electricity to you. After, you can watch a short film about electricity and safety.

☞ **SEASONS AND TIMES**
→ Summer: June—Aug, daily,
9:30 am—4 pm.
Winter: Sept—May, Mon—Fri,
9:30 am—4 pm; Sun, 1 pm—4 pm.

☞ **COST**
→ Free.

☞ **GETTING THERE**
→ By car, take the Champlain Bridge
south to Hwy. 10 S., continuing on to
Hwy. 30. Take Hwy. 30 north towards
Sorel to Exit 128 and follow the signs to
the Électrium. Free parking on site.
About 45 minutes from downtown.

☞ **COMMENT**
→ Plan a 1-hour visit.

☞ **SIMILAR ATTRACTION**
→ St. Lawrence-F.D.R. Power
Project Visitors' Center,
Massena, New York, (315) 764-0226,
www.nypa.gov/html/vcstlawr.html.

While the displays are intended to be educational and suited for children over 11, younger kids will enjoy pushing buttons to make lights go on and off, viewing the centre's pet electric eel and operating the Van de Graaff generator to make their hair stand on end.

Guided tours at the Électrium sometimes include visiting a nearby hydroelectric corridor.

CAPTAIN CATALYST

FRASER HICKSON LIBRARY
4855 AV. KENSINGTON (KENSINGTON AVE.)
MONTRÉAL
(514) 489-5301 OR 733-2048

Captain Catalyst, an interactive science program for kids 3 to 12, provides hands-on sessions (only in English) on such themes as chemistry, dinosaurs, the physics of toys, insects and mind-boggling puzzles. Educational workshops and birthday parties can be arranged. While you're at the library, check out the science playground in the auditorium. A scaled-down version can be transported to schools or daycare facilities.

☞ **SEASONS AND TIMES**
➤ Year-round: Schedule varies. Call for details.

☞ **COST**
➤ $5 per child for a 2-hour session. Group rates are available.

☞ **GETTING THERE**
➤ By car, take Hwy. 15 N. (Décarie Expressway) to Exit 66 and go west on Côte St. Luc Rd. Turn west onto Fielding Ave. until Kensington Ave. and go south. Free parking on site. About 10 minutes from downtown.
➤ By public transit, take the metro (orange line) to the Vendome station, board the 102 bus and get off at the corner of Madison Ave.

☞ **SIMILAR ATTRACTIONS**
➤ **Nomad Scientists**
(514) 481-3456
➤ **Mad Science Group**
(514) 344-4181 or 344-6691

Other Places to Learn

La Petite Grange
(chocolate shop and bakery)

415 CH. LAROCQUE (LAROCQUE RD.)
VALLEYFIELD
(450) 371-3510 OR (877) 371-3510

The Meury family, who have been running this chocolate factory and bakery since 1969, offer visitors a 45-minute guided tour of their small operation. You'll learn the difference between white and dark chocolate, watch sweets being made and, if you're lucky, see a demonstration of how to put creamy caramel inside a chocolate candy. Samples are generously provided.

☞ Summer: July—Aug, daily at 10 am and 2 pm.
Winter: Sept—June, Tue—Sat at 10 am and 2 pm.

☞ Tour: Adults $3, children $1.50, under 6 free, families $6 (prices include free samples).

☞ Take Hwy. 20 W. to Valleyfield (Exit 14) where you'll find posted blue signs to la Petite Grange. Free parking on site. About one hour from downtown.

Miron Quarry (city recycling centre)

2525 RUE JARRY E. (JARRY RD. E.)
MONTRÉAL
(514) 872-0761
WWW.VILLE.MONTREAL.QC.CA/PROPRETE/STMICHEL.HTM

Would you believe that garbage can be educational? At the Miron Quarry you can take a 90-minute guided tour to learn about recycling and waste management. Find out what happens to the contents of your recycling box by visiting the Sorting Centre for recyclable materials. The Composting Centre makes soil from dead leaves and discarded Christmas trees, and a thermal generating plant creates power from gases emanating from the dump. In addition there's a permanent exhibition on recycling solid wastes.

☞ Mon—Fri, 8 am—5 pm, by appointment only. Groups of 1 to 48 people can be accommodated.

☞ Free.

☞ Take St. Denis St. north to Jarry St. and go east to the Miron Quarry.
Take the metro (orange line) to the Jarry station. Board the 193 bus eastbound and get off at Iberville Rd.

Centre des Métiers du Verre du Québec (glass blowing workshop)

1200 RUE MILL (MILL RD.)
MONTRÉAL
(514) 933-6849
WWW.MTL.NET/~CMVQ

I n this converted fire hall you can watch glass blowers at work. Seeing artisans heating the glass until it's white hot and then blowing it into various shapes will fascinate everyone. If you like what you see, you may be able to buy it. The best time to visit the centre is during one of its periodic open houses. Call for the dates.

☞ Year-round: Mon—Fri, 8:30 am—noon, 1:30 pm—4:30 pm.

☞ Free.

☞ Take Peel St. south and turn west onto Wellington St., then south onto Bridge St. and west on Mill St.
Take the metro (orange line) to the Bonaventure station and take bus 107 down to Wellington St. Get off at the corner of Bridge St. and walk down Bridge to Mill St.

CHAPTER 7

MUSIC, THEATRE, DANCE AND CINEMA

Introduction

When we think of "culture vultures," we usually think of adults. But take your children to a play or concert at Place des Arts or to an open-air show put on by Legion River Theatre and you'll see that the love of the arts knows no age. Many theatres and cultural centres around town have regular presentations of music, variety, drama and dance that never fail to enchant younger audiences. This chapter contains a rundown of the venues that stage productions appropriate for kids. You'll also find an idea or two for places where children can receive instruction in the performing arts, including acting and hip hop. For movie buffs with a penchant for non-Hollywood films, we've provided the names of film festivals and other venues offering cinema for kids or families.

Don't forget your own neighbourhood. Your local Maison de la Culture (house of culture) offers art, dance, music and theatre at unbeatable prices for residents. These community centres are usually located beside the library or city hall. For a schedule of upcoming performances, ask your librarian or check the local newspaper.

The Sound of Music
MONTRÉAL SYMPHONY ORCHESTRA

175 RUE STE-CATHERINE O. (ST. CATHERINE ST. W.)
PLACE DES ARTS
MONTRÉAL
(514) 842-3402
WWW.INFOARTS.NET

The Montréal Symphony Orchestra has two special music programs for children. "Jeux d'enfants" (children's corner) is a series of public performances that introduces children ages 5 through 12 to classical music.

"Les matinées jeunesse" is an opera program available only to school groups. The productions are 90 minutes long and include bilingual animation and music.

☞ **SEASONS AND TIMES**
➤ For a schedule of performances, call the number above and ask for Judith de Repentigny.

☞ **COST**
➤ Jeux d'enfants: Adults $23, children $8.

☞ **GETTING THERE**
➤ By car, take Sherbrooke St. east to St. Urbain St. and turn south. Pay parking underground off St. Urbain between de Maisonneuve Blvd. and St. Catherine St.
➤ By public transit, take the metro (green line) to the Place-des-Arts station and follow the signs.

Kids' Concerts at
PLACE DES ARTS

175 RUE STE-CATHERINE O. (ST. CATHERINE ST. W.)
MONTRÉAL
(514) 285-4200 (INFORMATION) OR 842-2112 (TICKETS)
WWW.PDARTS.COM

☞ **SEASONS AND TIMES**
➤ MSO Concerts: Sun, 2:30 pm.
Son et brioches: Sun, 11 am.

☞ **GETTING THERE**
➤ By car, take Sherbrooke St. east to St. Urbain St. and turn south. Pay parking underground off St. Urbain between de Maisonneuve Blvd. and St. Catherine St.
➤ By public transit, take the metro (green line) to the Place-des-Arts station and follow the signs.

Place des Arts presents a series of Sunday afternoon kids' concerts in conjunction with the Montréal Symphony Orchestra (MSO). Call the centre to obtain a schedule, or look in the daily newspaper for a listing of upcoming shows. Place des Arts also puts on "sons et brioches." This popular family program features concerts and pastries. Arrive early if you hope to find any pastries left.

Grand Outings at
LA MAISON DES ARTS
DE LAVAL

1395 BOUL. DE LA CONCORDE O. (DE LA CONCORDE BLVD. W.)
LAVAL
(450) 662-9564 (INFORMATION) OR 667-2040 (TICKETS)
WWW.RIDEAU-INC.QC.CA/DIFFUSE/FICHE/77.HTM

The Maison des Arts' "Grandes sorties, jeune public" program is a series of performances in French that includes plays, concerts and puppetry. Some of the shows are suitable for children as young as four and many are followed by family workshops.

On Sunday mornings, the public can attend "les déjeuners croissant-musique," which feature a breakfast of pastries, coffee and juice followed by an hour-long concert. Call 687-3987 for information.

☞ **SEASONS AND TIMES**
→ Grandes sorties: Late Oct—late May. Call for dates and times.
Déjeuners croissant-musique: Late Oct—late May, Sun, 10 am.

☞ **COST**
→ Grandes Sorties: $9 (some shows may be more).
Workshops: Adults free, children $5.
Déjeuners croissant-musique:
Adults $11.50, children under 6 $6.
Discounts for Laval residents.

☞ **GETTING THERE**
→ By car, take Hwy. 15 N. to the first exit in Laval and follow the signs for de la Concorde Blvd. Look for the blue signs directing you to la Maison des Arts. Free parking on site. About 25 minutes from downtown.
→ By public transit, take the metro (orange line) to the Henri-Bourassa station, then board STL bus 40.

Taking Centre Stage at THE SAIDYE BRONFMAN CENTRE FOR THE ARTS

5170 CH. DE LA CÔTE-STE-CATHERINE (CÔTE ST. CATHERINE RD.)
MONTRÉAL
(514) 739-2301 OR 739-7944 (TICKETS)
WWW.THESAIDYE.ORG

☞ **SEASONS AND TIMES**
➤ The Centre is open year-round, but programming is seasonal. Call for schedule.

☞ **COST**
➤ Artapalooza: $6.
Classes, camps and workshops: varies with the program. Financial assistance is sometimes made available for those in need.

☞ **GETTING THERE**
➤ By car, take Guy St. north (it becomes Côte des Neiges) and continue to Côte St. Catherine, then go west.
➤ By public transit, take the metro (orange line) to the Côte Ste. Catherine station and walk west.

☞ **NEARBY**
➤ St. Joseph's Oratory, Mount Royal Park.

☞ **SIMILAR ATTRACTION**
➤ **Visual Arts Centre**, 350 Victoria Ave., Westmount, (514) 488-9558.

In addition to producing a vibrant adult theatrical schedule in English, French and sometimes Yiddish (check the current schedule for shows that might appeal to your children), the Saidye Bronfman Centre offers Artapalooza, an annual festival of the performing arts for children and teenagers held in late January and early February. Music, puppet shows and plays (some by teenage actors) are each followed by free public workshops.

The Saidye also boasts a youth institute that offers classes in painting, drama, drawing, cartooning, hip hop and more. There is an artistic daycamp for kids ages 5 to 12 during the summer and winter school holidays with drama, dance, painting and musical theatre on the agenda. School groups of all ages are invited to A Day at the Saidye, a hands-on workshop featuring painting, puppets, or theatre. Half-day programs start at $7 a child. Alternatively, professional artists from the Saidye will visit schools to conduct workshops.

French Children's Plays at LA MAISON THÉÂTRE

255 RUE ONTARIO E. (ONTARIO ST. E.)
MONTRÉAL
(514) 288-7211 OR 1-800-361-4595

Possibly the best children's theatre in Montréal, La Maison Théâtre stages a dozen or so performances each year that are aimed at 4 to 12 year-olds. From October through May, there are weekday performances for school groups and weekend performances for the public, which usually begin at 3 pm. Other events offered here include dance, workshops and "parole aux enfants" discussions.

☞ **SEASONS AND TIMES**
➤ Call for the current schedule of events.

☞ **COST**
➤ Adults $15, children $11.

☞ **GETTING THERE**
➤ By car, take Sherbrooke St. east to Clarke St. Go south on Clarke to Ontario St., then turn east.
➤ By public transit, take the metro (green or orange lines) to the Berri-UQAM station, exit rue St. Denis and go north to Ontario St. and then west along Ontario.

English Children's Plays at THE CENTAUR THEATRE

453 RUE ST-FRANÇOIS-XAVIER (ST. FRANÇOIS XAVIER ST.)
MONTRÉAL
(514) 288-3161

☞ **SEASONS AND TIMES**
➤ Oct—May, Sat, 10:30 am. Call for the current schedule.

☞ **COST**
➤ Adults $5, children $3.

☞ **GETTING THERE**
➤ By car, take René-Lévesque Blvd. to Beaver Hall Hill and turn south (it becomes McGill St.). Turn east on Notre Dame St., south on St. Jean St. and east on l'Hôpital St. Pay parking on l'Hôpital. The theatre is on the next corner. Minutes from downtown.
➤ By public transit, take the metro (orange line) to the Place-d'Armes station and walk south on St. François Xavier. Or, take the 55 bus south from the Saint-Laurent metro station (green line) and exit at St. Urbain and Notre Dame streets.

N o need to be glued to the tube Saturday morning when you can see a play instead. Centaur Theatre offers plays for children ages 5 to 12, put on by various theatre companies on selected Saturday mornings during the school year.

The Centaur also runs a program for school groups entitled "Theatre of Tomorrow." Children can attend a play and afterwards meet the cast members.

Other Children's Theatres

H ere is a partial listing of some of Montréal's other children's theatres. Call the individual theatres, or the Québec Drama Federation (514-843-8698), for more information.

THÉÂTRE DE L'ESQUISSE
1650 RUE MARIE-ANNE E. (MARIE ANNE ST. E.)
MONTRÉAL
MONT-ROYAL METRO, BUS 97 EAST

T his small east end theatre puts on weekend performances (mostly in French) for audiences ages 3 to 12. Reservations required. Tickets start at $7.

OXYJEUNE
420 RUE ST-PAUL E. (ST. PAUL ST. E.)
MONTRÉAL
(514) 849-5297

QUÉBEC THEATRE CENTRE
FOR CHILDREN AND YOUTH
255 RUE ONTARIO E. (ONTARIO ST. E.)
MONTRÉAL
(514) 288-7211
BERRI-UQAM METRO; EXIT RUE ST-DENIS

P resents French-language theatre on weekdays at schools; public performances on weekends at the theatre.

☞ Schools: Oct—May, Tue—Fri, 10 am and 1:30 pm.
Public: Sat—Sun, 1 pm and 3 pm.

RENDEZ-VOUS INTERNATIONAL
DE THÉÂTRE JEUNE PUBLIC
260 BOUL. DE MAISONNEUVE O. (DE MAISONNEUVE BLVD. W.)
PLACE DES ARTS
MONTRÉAL
(514) 499-2929
PLACE-DES-ARTS METRO

TRICYCLE PRODUCTIONS
(514) 369-4968
HTTP://NETROVER.COM/~TRICYCLE

This roving theatre company visits schools and puts on performances in English for children aged 4 to 12.

MONTRÉAL SCHOOL OF PERFORMING ARTS/EXPRESSO THEATRE
3480 BOUL. DÉCARIE (DÉCARIE BLVD.), 2ND FLOOR
MONTRÉAL
(514) 483-5526

This training-school for young English-speaking actors puts on plays for children in December. The theatre's schedule also includes performances for older audiences between April and October. Workshops are available for aspiring actors and there are occasional drama field trips to New York City.

☞ Tickets start at $5.

SHAKESPEARE IN THE PARK

REPERCUSSION THEATRE (514) 495-8875
LEGION RIVER THEATRE (514) 845-9607

What better way to introduce children to live theatre than by experiencing it in the open air. Attending performances of Shakespeare's plays on a summer evening has become a tradition for many Montréal families. Grab a blanket or bring a lawn chair. The shows take place under the stars, often beginning at dusk. Why not go earlier and have a picnic before watching the show.

Performances given by the Legion River Theatre take place in Mount Royal Park near the Cartier Monument on Park Avenue. The Repercussion Theatre stages plays in city parks around the Island of Montréal.

☞ **SEASONS AND TIMES**
➤ Mount Royal Park: July, 7 pm–9 pm.
Elsewhere: Late summer, 8:30 pm–10:30 pm.
(Call the theatre companies for exact dates and locations of their performances.)

☞ **COST**
➤ Free. Donations are accepted.

☞ **COMMENT**
➤ The Legion River Theatre plays are processional. (The audience follows the actors as they move around the park.) English performances only.

MOVIE LIBRARIES

NATIONAL FILM BOARD CINEMA
1564 RUE ST-DENIS (ST. DENIS ST.)
MONTRÉAL
(514) 496-6887
WWW.NFB.CA/E/CINEROBOTHEQUE
BERRI-UQAM METRO

Visit the world's only CinéRobothèque, where a robot helps you to select the film you want to see. Thousands of National Film Board (NFB) titles are available, and there is a good collection of NFB children's films too. Groups can take advantage of the hourly rates.

☞ Year-round: Tue—Sun, noon—9 pm.
Groups: Mon—Fri, 9 am—9 pm; weekends 10 am—9 pm.

☞ Adults $3 per hour, students and seniors $2 per hour.
Video theatre rental: Starting at $15 per hour.
Cinema rental: Starting at $50 per hour.
Video rental: $3 per video per day.

QUÉBEC FILM LIBRARY AND CINEMA MUSEUM
335 BOUL. DE MAISONNEUVE E. (DE MAISONNEUVE BLVD. E.)
MONTRÉAL
(514) 842-9763
WWW.CINEMATHEQUE.QC.CA
BERRI-UQAM METRO

T wo screenings every day from the library's collection of over 28,000 (mainly Québec-produced) films. Under the same roof, the Cinema Museum has movie posters and photographs, film projectors, cameras, sets, and props for film buffs to pore over.

☞ Exhibits: Year-round, Tue—Sun, 1 pm—6 pm (Wed until 8 pm).
Films: Year-round, Tue—Fri, 1 pm—8 pm.

☞ Films or exhibits: Adults $4, children (6 to 15) $2, under 6 free.
For both: Adults $6, children (6 to 15) $3, under 6 free.
Free admission to exhibits on Wed, 6—8 pm.

Seeing the Big Picture
IMAX™ FILMS

You haven't enjoyed a big-screen experience until you've seen a movie at an IMAX™ theatre. Its seven-storey projection screen places every audience member

☞ **SEASONS AND TIMES**
➤ Year-round: Call for show times.

☞ **COST**
➤ Prices vary with the program but expect to pay between $8 and $12 per person.

at the centre of the action. Whether you're watching a feature on the pyramids or a documentary following climbers up Mount Everest, when the film begins you'll be glued to your seat. And Montréal has not one, but three of these behemoth screens.

OLD PORT IMAX™
KING EDWARD PIER
MONTRÉAL
(514) 496-4629
WWW.IMAXOLDPORT.COM
PLACE D'ARMES METRO

PARAMOUNT IMAX™
977 RUE STE-CATHERINE O. (ST. CATHERINE ST. W.)
MONTRÉAL
(514) 878-9100
WWW.FAMOUSPLAYERSMOVIES.COM/IMAXINDEX.HTML
PEEL METRO

IMAX™ LES AILES
2153, BOUL. LAPINIÈRE (LAPINIÈRE BLVD.)
MAIL CHAMPLAIN (CHAMPLAIN MALL)
BROSSARD
(450) 672-4629
WWW.IMAX.COM/THEATRES/BROSSARD.HTML

Children's Film
FESTIVALS

G ot a budding film critic in your family? Why not take in a children's film festival, or better yet, two.

LES 400 COUPS

RENDEZ-VOUS INTERNATIONAL DE CINÉMA JEUNE PUBLIC
260 BOUL. DE MAISONNEUVE O. (DE MAISONNEUVE BLVD. W.)
MONTRÉAL
(514) 499-2929
WWW.LES400COUPS.COM

F or the past five years, Rendez-vous International has run a children's film festival in conjunction with the Cinémathèque québécoise and the National Film Board. Designed for kids from 4 to 16, the festival shows films in French and English with children as the judges. Formerly held in April, les 400 Coups now runs in the fall.

If you missed last year's festival you can catch the five best films over five Sundays from January to May at Ciné-Kid, Ex-Centris, 3536 St. Laurent Blvd. Call (514) 847-2206 or surf over to www.ex-centris.com for more information.

Rendez-vous International also hosts "des Coups de Théâtre," an extravaganza of music, theatre and dance for young people in late May and early June. Call for more information.

☞ $4 per person per film.

MONTRÉAL INTERNATIONAL CHILDREN'S FILM FESTIVAL

CINÉMA IMPÉRIAL
1430 RUE DE BLEURY (BLEURY ST.)
MONTRÉAL
(514) 848-0300 (GENERAL) OR 848-7187 (INFORMATION)

The Cinéma Impérial holds an annual film festival during the March school break for kids ages 3 to 12. The public is invited to sit on a cyber jury to select the best films.

☞ Daily screenings at 10 am and 1 pm.

☞ Tickets start at $4.

CHAPTER 8

Animals, Farms & Zoos

Introduction

One of the best things about Montréal is that you can visit the countryside without leaving the island. There are farms located right in the city where your family can see a dairy herd being milked, have a tractor ride or walk through a barnyard full of pigs, chickens, sheep and other farm critters.

In the spring, join the centuries-old Québec tradition of celebrating the making of maple syrup. Visit a "cabane à sucre" and eat taffy off the snow! A short drive from downtown and across the river takes you into the apple-growing heartland of Québec. What better activity for a fall family outing than to pick delicious, crunchy apples? Don't worry strawberry lovers, there are suggestions in this chapter for you, too.

The Ecomuseum has native species such as wolves and deer. But if that's too tame for you, visit the Exotarium Reptile Farm or the Granby Zoo, which are full of animals from all over the world, from the cute and furry to the creepy crawly.

So make your plans, pack up your van and head out for a day of family fun.

Places to
PICK APPLES

(514) 873-2015 TOURISME QUÉBEC

What could taste better than a McIntosh apple picked straight from the tree? Montréalers are doubly fortunate because our cold climate enhances the apples' sought-after sharp taste and the bulk of Québec's apple-growing industry is concentrated nearby.

Many area apple growers welcome the public to their orchards to pick apples. Plan to make a day

> ☞ **SEASONS AND TIMES**
> ➤ Aug—late Oct.
>
> ☞ **COST**
> ➤ About $0.65 per kilogram.
> Interpretation centre: Adults $2.

of your outing and take a picnic to eat under the trees. Call ahead before you go. Some orchards have no facilities. Others offer a full range of services including areas for picnics, washrooms, gift centres, snack bars, tractor rides and fresh farm produce.

Look for orchards advertising "arrosage minimale." They use pesticides sparingly on their trees. Depending on the apple variety and that year's growing conditions, apple-picking season usually runs from late August to late October.

Why not also visit the orchards at the end of May, when the apple blossoms are at their peak? To learn about the history and cultivation of apples, visit the Apple Interpretation Centre in Rougemont (May to October, 10 am to 5 pm, 450-469-3600). Mont St. Hilaire has an apple museum that's open year-round (450-446-2552).

These popular apple-picking sites are located within one hour of Montréal.

BOLDUC ORCHARD
4305 RG. DU HAUT-ST-FRANÇOIS
LAVAL
(450) 661-3025

QUINN FARM (PAGE 157)
2495 BOUL. PERROT S.
ÎLE-PERROT
(514) 453-1510

You'll see the apple orchards as you approach the towns and villages below. Look for signs along the roadside that read "Auto cueuillette" or "Cueuillez-vous même."

COVEY HILL
HWY. 15 S., EXIT 6, RTE. 202 W.
(450) 454-5115

FRELIGHSBURG
HWY. 10 E., EXIT 68, RTES, 139 S., 202 W., 213 S.

MONT-ST-BRUNO
HWY. 20 E., EXIT 98 TO HWY. 30 S., EXIT 121.

MONT-ST-HILAIRE
HWY. 20 E., EXIT 137.
(450) 446-2552

MONT-ST-GREGOIRE
HWY. 10 E., EXIT 37.

ROUGEMONT
HWY. 10 E., EXIT 48.
(450) 469-3600

ST-JOSEPH-DU-LAC
HWY. 640 W., EXIT 2.
(450) 491-1991

Walk with the Animals at
THE ECOMUSEUM

21125 CH. STE-MARIE (ST. MARIE RD.)
STE-ANNE-DE-BELLEVUE
(514) 457-9449

A few hours at the Ecomuseum will delight any family that cherishes animals. This wildlife observation centre has over 90 species native to the St. Lawrence Valley that the public can view.

Walking trails and boardwalks will lead you through meadows, around swamp and over gently rolling woodland where white-tailed deer, caribou, raccoons, lynx, wolves, snakes, turtles and many other creatures are found. Biologists are on-hand to answer questions.

Don't miss the birds of prey exhibit. Its feathered denizens include snowy owls, golden eagles and peregrine falcons. Visit the walk-in aviary and the butterfly garden as well.

You'll find nature-related exhibits as well as hands-on displays at the Ecomuseum's education building and in the welcome centre. The Ecomuseum has a frog hunt in

☞ **SEASONS AND TIMES**
➤ Year-round: Daily, 9 am–4 pm. Closed Christmas Day.

☞ **COST**
➤ Adults $5, seniors $4, children (5 to 14) $3, under 5 free.

☞ **GETTING THERE**
➤ By car, take Hwy. 40 W. to Exit 41 and follow the signs to Ste. Marie Rd. Turn east and continue on to the Ecomuseum. It's on the left. Free parking on site. About 30 minutes from downtown.
➤ By public transit, call the STCUM (288-6287) for information.
➤ By bicycle, follow the Lachine Canal bike path and continue along Lakeshore Rd. to Macdonald College. Bike across the campus to Ste. Marie Rd. and go east.

☞ **NEARBY**
➤ Morgan Arboretum, Cap St. Jacques Regional Park.

> ☞ **COMMENT**
> ➤ You can sponsor animals at the Ecomuseum. Plan a 2-hour visit.
>
> ☞ **SIMILAR ATTRACTIONS**
> ➤ **Papanack Animal Farm**
> 150 Nine Mile Creek, Wendover, Ontario (W. of Hawkesbury)
> (613) 673-7225

April and activities around Easter and Halloween. Children's birthday parties and sleepovers are offered.

Slithering through
THE EXOTARIUM
REPTILE FARM

846 RG. FRESNIÈRE (FRESNIÈRE ROW)
FRESNIÈRE (NEAR ST-EUSTACHE)
(450) 472-1827

Visiting this farm is not for the faint of heart; still some kids will probably be thrilled to have a big, hairy tarantula crawl up their arm. Of course, you don't have to play with spiders or any of the other creepy crawlies that are on display. The Exotarium has more than 50 different types of reptiles and other animals, including giant pythons, iguanas, alligators, caimans, Gila monsters, snakes, turtles and brightly-coloured tropical frogs.

Outdoors, there is a pond with crocodiles. Bring some change for

> ☞ **SEASONS AND TIMES**
> ➤ Summer: July—Aug, Thu—Tue, noon—5 pm.
> Regular: Sept—mid-Dec and Feb—June, Fri—Sun, noon—5 pm.
>
> ☞ **COST**
> ➤ Adults $5, children $3.50, family and group rates available.

the feed machine and you can toss them food. The farm has animal demonstrations regularly. After, hold a lizard or a snake if you dare!

☞ **GETTING THERE**
➤ By car, take Hwy. 640 W. to Exit 8 and follow the signs for Intermiel. Cross the railway tracks and begin looking for a white building on the left-hand side with lizards painted on it. About seven kilometres from the 640. Free parking on site. About 55 minutes from downtown.

☞ **NEARBY**
➤ Intermiel bee hives.

☞ **COMMENT**
➤ No steps, but narrow aisles, so strollers can be tricky. There's apple picking at the Exotarium's orchard in the fall. Plan a 90-minute visit.

Animal Crackers at THE GRANBY ZOO

347 RUE BOURGET (BOURGET RD.)
GRANBY
(450) 372-9113 OR 1-877-472-6290
WWW.ZOOGRANBY.QC.CA

Plan to make a day of your visit to the Granby Zoo. The centre, which is home to nearly 1,000 animals, from apes to zebras and exotic birds to reptiles and amphibians, features a children's park, an amusement

☞ **SEASONS AND TIMES**
➤ Summer: Mid-June—Labour Day, daily, 10 am—5 pm.
Autumn: Labour Day—Thanksgiving, Sat—Sun, 10 am—5 pm.

☞ **COST**
➤ Adults $19.95, students $13.95, children $8.95, families $59.95.

☞ **GETTING THERE**

→ By car, take the Champlain Bridge to Hwy. 10 and go east towards Sherbrooke. Take Exit 68, and follow Rte. 139 N. (David Bouchard Blvd.) to the zoo. It's on the right. Free parking on site. About one hour from downtown.

☞ **NEARBY**

→ Exotic Bird Zoo (page 223)

park, a water park and other fun attractions as well.

Paved trails will lead you to such exhibits as the African Pavilion, which has the ever-popular lions and gorillas, the reptile house and the feline pavilion. If your kids want to reach out and touch an animal, make sure you wait until the petting farm. Camel rides and train rides are also offered and children can have their faces painted. Extra charges apply.

There are plenty of benches scattered throughout the zoo, and while some are shaded, make sure everyone is wearing sunscreen. At mealtime you'll find restaurants on site. The zoo rents carts and strollers, or you can bring your own from home.

Mosey over to
THE MACDONALD AGRICULTURAL FARM

21111 CH. LAKESHORE (LAKESHORE RD.)
STE-ANNE-DE-BELLEVUE
(514) 398-7701
WWW.TOTAL.NET/~MACFARM

I f your kids believe that milk comes from stores, maybe it's time they saw a dairy cow. They can visit a whole herd at the Macdonald

Agricultural Farm. The farm, which is part of the Macdonald Agricultural College, is open for visits from the public daily. Summer is the best time to visit as that's when you'll get to see the other critters, such as ducks, geese, goats, rabbits, sheep and turkeys outside in the barnyard. Call ahead and inquire when the cows are milked. Kids and adults alike will be fascinated by the operation.

There is also a small museum devoted to agriculture with a model farm tractor to inspect. School groups can arrange to go on a one-hour educational visit. Call 398-7701 or fax 398-8134 for more information.

Try to visit on a dry, sunny day. The barnyard can be muddy. When you go, take along a Frisbee™ or a ball. There's plenty of room to run and play.

☞ **SEASONS AND TIMES**
➤ Year-round: Daily, 11:30 am—3 pm.

☞ **COST**
➤ Individuals: Free.
Groups: $3 per person.

☞ **GETTING THERE**
➤ By car, take Hwy. 40 W. to Exit 41 (Ste. Anne) and follow the signs for Ste. Marie Rd. Turn west at the first stop, and south at the second. The farm is on your right.
By public transit, take the 211 bus from the Lionel-Groulx metro station to the end of the line (it's a very long ride). Or, take the Rigaud commuter train to Ste. Anne de Bellevue station and ride the minibus to Macdonald College.

☞ **NEARBY**
➤ Morgan Arboretum, Ecomuseum, Quinn Farm, Lyman Entomological Museum.

The Sweet Taste of Summer
PLACES TO PICK
STRAWBERRIES

(514) 873-2015 TOURISME QUÉBEC

Strawberries never taste better than when eaten straight from the plant on a warm summer day. And that's what you get to do when you go strawberry picking. The season usually begins in the third week of June and lasts about a month, though some farms produce a second crop later in the summer.

The strawberry varieties grown in Québec are small, but they're bursting with flavour. Luckily, there's no shortage of farms nearby where you can pick your own. Like apple orchards, however, the facilities at each farm vary between locations. Some have tractor rides and on-site restaurants, while others provide only baskets and fields of berries. Remember to bring hats and sunscreen for everyone as the fields are in full sun.

These strawberry farms are within an hour of Montréal. The fields are easy to spot as you approach the areas, and there are often Québec Highway blue signs to guide you to them.

☞ **SEASONS AND TIMES**
➡ Late June—late July: Daily, 10 am—7 pm.

☞ **COST**
➡ Pay by the kilogram. What you eat in the fields is free.

☞ **COMMENT**
➡ The Scottish names Fraser and Frazier are derived from the French word fraisier, or strawberry farmer.

BLAINVILLE
HWY. 15 N., EXIT 25.

ÎLE-PERROT
HWY. 20 W.

OKA
HWY. 640 W.

STE-ANNE-DES-PLAINES
RTE. 335 N.

ST-HUBERT
HWY. 30 AND RTE. 112
(450) 445-6375

ST-JOSEPH-DU-LAC
HWY. 640 W.

STE-MADELEINE
HWY. 20 E., EXIT 120.

A Taste of the Past
SUGAR BUSHES
(Cabanes à sucre)

(514) 873-2015 TOURISME QUÉBEC

C ome late winter, when the sap starts to flow from Québec's maple trees, families make their plans to attend sugaring-off parties. Highlighted by good food, much merriment and lots of maple syrup, the lively celebrations continue a tradition that is centuries old.

Native peoples from the Great Lakes and St. Lawrence regions were making maple syrup long before the Europeans arrived. Later, they showed French settlers how to tap the trees, collect the sap and reduce it to syrup. It's a laborious task—after hours of boiling, 40 litres of watery sap produce just one litre of syrup. The settlers also learned to celebrate the job's completion with a party. They square-danced, went for sleigh rides, prepared large banquets and poured steaming syrup onto the snow to make taffy.

Today, plastic piping and mechanized production have replaced the wooden buckets of yesteryear, but the celebration endures. Why not join in the festivities at one of these "cabanes à sucre" near Montréal?

PHILIPPE LALONDE
1535 RUE PERROT
ÎLE-PERROT (HWY. 20 O.)
(514) 453-8414
(MAR—APR)

SUCRERIE À L'ORÉE DU BOIS
11381 RG. LA FRESNIÈRE
MIRABEL (RTE. 148)
(450) 258-2976
(YEAR-ROUND WITH RESERVATION)

CABANE À SUCRE CONSTANTIN
1054 BOUL. ARTHUR-SAUVÉ
ST-EUSTACHE (RTE. 148)
(450) 473-2374
(YEAR-ROUND WITH RESERVATION)

SUCRERIE DE LA MONTAGNE
300 RG. ST-GEORGES
RIGAUD (RTE. 325)
(450) 451-0831
(YEAR-ROUND, TOURS, DANCING, MUSIC)

ERABLIÈRE MONT ROUGE
540 DU MOULIN
ROUGEMONT
(450) 469-2221
(YEAR-ROUND)

ERABLIÈRE LE ROSSIGNOL
30 MONTÉE DES QUARANTE-DEUX (HWY. 20 E.)
STE-JULIE
(450) 649-2020
(MAR—APR)

JACQUES GREGOIRE
115 RG. DES PINS
ST-ESPRIT (RTE. 25)
(450) 831-2350
(YEAR-ROUND)

ÉRABLIÈRE RAYMOND MEUNIER ET FILS
325 RANG DES CINQUANTE-QUATRE
RICHELIEU (HWY. 10 E.)
(450) 347-0757
(MAR-APR, TOURS, DANCING, MUSIC)

Pick of the Crop at
QUINN FARM

2495 BOUL. PERROT S. (PERROT BLVD. S.)
ÎLE-PERROT
(514) 453-1510

You can drive your kids to see a real working farm in less time than it takes to watch an episode of Sesame Street. However, who has time to work with hay rides to go on, animals to see, kites to fly and corn roasts to attend?

You can pick your own fruits and vegetables at the farm. In-season delights include strawberries, blueberries, gooseberries, currants, apples, sweet corn and pumpkins. Special activities for

☞ **SEASONS AND TIMES**
→ Year-round. Call ahead to verify times of activities.

☞ **COST**
→ Varies with the activity.

☞ **GETTING THERE**
→ By car, take Hwy. 20 W. to Île Perrot, turn left onto Don Quichotte Blvd. and follow the signs to the farm. Free parking on site. About 35 minutes from downtown.

☞ **NEARBY**
→ Pointe du Moulin Park.

kids include videos and slide shows about agriculture, a theatre and birthday parties. There's no shortage of things to do during wintertime either. Why not bundle the family up and take them skating or cross-country skiing?

Quinn's has a family brunch before Christmas that includes a sleigh ride, and a tree to take home. There's also a regular brunch that's served on Sundays at the on-site restaurant. Don't forget to drop by the bakery at the farm. You won't leave empty-handed.

Mending Broken Wings at LE NICHOIR *(Bird Rehabilitation Centre)*

637 CH. MAIN (MAIN RD.)
HUDSON
(450) 458-2809

☞ **SEASONS AND TIMES**
→ June–Aug, Wed, 4 pm–6 pm; Sun, 2 pm–4 pm, weather permitting. Group visits by appointment only.

☞ **COST**
→ Adults $2, under 12 free.

☞ **GETTING THERE**
→ By car, take Hwy. 720 W. to Hwy. 15 N. and continue on to Hwy. 40 W. (Trans-Canada Hwy.). Take Exit 22 for Hudson. Turn north onto St Charles St. and continue to the end, turning west on Main Rd. Look for the sign on your left. Free parking on site. About 50 minutes from downtown.

☞ **COMMENT**
→ Plan a 30-minute visit.

☞ **SIMILAR ATTRACTIONS**
→ **Chouette à Voir**.
A bird rehabilitation centre specializing in raptors near St. Hyacinthe, (450) 345-8521 ext. 8545.

Since 1994, le Nichoir has been operating a rehabilitation centre for injured and orphaned birds, and providing a telephone help line. Over 1000 birds are brought here by the public each year; most of them are eventually released into the wild.

The best time to visit is during one of the two open houses the centre holds in June and August. The old barn is filled with baby warblers, thrushes, chickadees, blue jays, ducks, and woodpeckers. Special activities include guided nature walks, bird of prey demonstrations, story telling and a hot dog roast.

This is mainly an indoor site, although there are some aviaries in the field behind the barn. The

injured birds are easily startled by loud noises or sud-
den movements,

Other Places to Visit

The Little Farm at Angrignon Park

3400 BOUL. DES TRINITAIRES (TRINITAIRES BLVD.)
MONTRÉAL
(514) 872-4689
WWW.VILLE.MONTREAL.QC.CA/JARDIN/FERME/FERME.HTM

I deal for the younger set, the Little Farm is geared
toward city children who have never seen farm animal before. Kids will be thrilled to get up close to
chickens, cows, donkeys, ducks and sheep. The farm
also has emus, llamas, peacocks, pheasants, and
pigeons. There are coin-operated machines with food
for the animals so bring along some change and you
can feed the goats and sheep. Animators are on hand to
present different farm themes, mainly in French, to
young children every week.

☞ Early July–Labour Day: Daily, 9:30 am–5 pm.

☞ Free.

☞ Take Hwy. 15 S. to Exit 62 and continue on de la Vérendrye
Blvd. Turn north on des Trinitaires Blvd. and follow the signs for
parking at the metro station. A large yellow sign marks the farm's
entrance. Pay parking on weekdays, free on weekends.
Take the metro (green line) to the Angrignon station and walk
across the parking lot.

Parc Safari

850 RTE. 202
HEMMINGFORD
(450) 247-2727 OR 1-800-465-8724
WWW.PARCSAFARI.COM

Whether you want to walk or drive through the wilds of Parc Safari, your kids will love the experience. This family recreational park features animals from around the world, a water park, amusement rides, animal rides, shows, picnic sites, restaurants and more. To beat the crowds, do the walk-through part first, saving the drive-through safari for later in the day when everyone else is at the amusement park. Bring carrots if you want to feed the animals. The park does sell boxes of food pellets, however the animals prefer fresh veggies.

☞ Mid-May—Sept: Daily, 10 am—4:30 pm.

☞ Adults $19.99, seniors (55 plus) and children (3 to 10) $13.91, under 3 free. Maximum car price (for seven people) is $69.55. This price covers everything except tube rental for the water area, elephant rides and pony rides. Credit cards and Interac accepted.

☞ Take Hwy. 15 S. to Rte. 202, go west and watch for the signs directing you to the site.

The Ecological Farm

CAP-ST-JACQUES REGIONAL PARK
190 CH. DU CAP-ST-JACQUES (CAP ST. JACQUES RD.)
PIERREFONDS
(514) 280-6743
WWW.D3PIERRES.QC.CA (FRENCH)
WWW.CUM.QC.CA/PARCS-NATURE (FRENCH AND ENGLISH)

This organic farm features a barnyard filled with friendly critters such as cows, ducks, goats, horses, chickens, pigs and turkeys. You'll learn all about them if you go on the guided tour ($5 per person). Cap St. Jacques also offers nature interpretation, in-season tractor and sleigh rides, an obstacle course, a harvest festival in August and storytelling with puppets in the winter. The farm is ideal for picnics, or dine in the restaurant at the old farmhouse. Bring your bicycles or cross-country skis depending on the season.

☞   Spring—Fall: Daily, 10 am—5 pm.

☞   Free.

☞   Take Hwy. 40 W. to St. Charles Blvd. (Exit 50) and go north until Gouin Blvd., then turn west. Continue on until you see the signs for the park. Once there, stay on Cap St. Jacques Rd. and follow the signs to the farm. Parking $4.
Call the STCUM (288-6287) for information about using public transit.

CHAPTER 9

green spaces

Introduction

P arks are natural destinations for family outings. Fortunately, Montréal has many fine
parks where you and your kids can picnic in
the shade of old trees, kick around a ball, enjoy the
scenery and generally get away from it all. But some
parks provide opportunities of a more exciting variety. At Mount Royal Park you can visit the police
stables or go downhill skiing. Parc-des-Îles boasts
a Formula One racetrack. At René-Lévesque Park
you can stroll through an outdoor sculpture museum. And if you've always wanted to try camping, Oka
Park has just the site for you—they'll even rent you
the necessary equipment. Parks allow you to create
your own fun, and at the end of the day, that's what
family outings are all about.

The Mountain
MOUNT ROYAL PARK
(Beaver Lake Sector)

VOIE CAMILLIEN-HOUDE (CAMILLIEN HOUDE WAY)
MONTRÉAL
(514) 872-6559
WWW.VILLE.MONTREAL.QC.CA/PARCS

Montréal's most famous park is also one of its best. Perched 200 metres above the heart of the city, the "mountain" dominates the local topography and is as much a refuge for families getting away from it all as it is for many species of wildlife.

The park's Beaver Lake section is popular with families. Kids can ride a pedal boat on the lake, run along wooded trails, explore in the play area and see police officers on horseback. The MUC stables (1515 Camillien Houde) are open to the public and you can watch the horses being fed and groomed.

In wintertime, the park becomes a wonderland featuring sleigh rides, skating on the lake,

☞ **SEASONS AND TIMES**
➔ Year-round. Some activities are seasonal.
Maison Smith Museum: Year-round, daily, 10 am—5 pm.

☞ **COST**
➔ Free. Fee for some activities.

☞ **GETTING THERE**
➔ By car, take Sherbrooke St. W. to Côte des Neiges Rd. Go north on Côte des Neiges to Remembrance Rd. and turn east. You can also access the eastern section of the park via Camillien Houde Way. Follow the signs for pay parking.
➔ By public transit, take the metro (orange line) to the Mont-Royal station, and board the 11 bus to Beaver Lake.
➔ By bicycle, follow the Rachel St. bike path across Park Ave. and into the park. Continue past the Cartier monument and up Olmsted Rd. (no cars allowed). It's a long, steep climb.

☞ **COMMENT**
➔ The cross-country ski trails are challenging.

cross-country skiing, tobogganing and much more. There's even a free tow for the downhill skiing site.

The Maison Smith Museum, higher up the mountain, has exhibits on local geology, ecology and history for viewing. School groups can arrange to have a guided nature tour or have a naturalist visit the class (843-8240). In the summer, the Friends of the Mountain offer ecology tours (844-4928). Be sure you visit the lookout, which offers a spectacular view of Montréal and the St. Lawrence River.

Sunny Days
WESTMOUNT PARK

4574 rue Sherbrooke O. (Sherbrooke St. W.)
Westmount
(514) 989-5353

This may be the best children's park in Montréal. A sandy play area has everything kids need for swinging, sliding, digging and climbing and there are cannons nearby for investigating.

A gazebo, soccer fields and a wading pool for toddlers are a short stroll from the playground and an artificial stream, complete with waterfalls, meanders through part of the site. The park's terrain is mostly level so little kids can run around without stumbling, and towering trees create welcome

☞ **SEASONS AND TIMES**
→ Year-round: Daily, dawn to dusk.
Call 989-5353 to obtain a Westmount Park schedule.

☞ **COST**
→ Free.

retreats from the sun on hot days. On certain summer evenings, outdoor theatre is performed here. Bring lawn chairs and a blanket for the kids to cozy up in.

The Westmount Public Library and the municipal greenhouses are found near the play area. They're a good alternative to the park if the weather is not so fine.

☞ **GETTING THERE**

➤ By car, take Sherbrooke St. west to Melville Ave. Free parking on nearby streets.

➤ By public transit, take the metro (green line) to the Atwater station and board the 138 or 104 bus. Get off at the Westmount Public Library. The 24 bus also stops here.

➤ By bicycle, follow the de Maisonneuve bicycle path to Westmount Park.

☞ **NEARBY**

➤ Westmount YMCA, Vendome commuter train and metro station.

Fun for all Seasons
PARC-DES-ÎLES

Île-Ste-Hélène
Montréal
(514) 872-4537

Parc-des-Îles is Montréal's largest city park and a popular family destination. Little wonder. The site, which is located on Ste. Hélène and Notre Dame islands, boasts

☞ **SEASONS AND TIMES**

➤ Year-round. Call 872-4537 for the times of specific activities.

☞ **COST**

➤ Admission to the park: Free. Parking $7.50.
Beach: Adults $6, children $2.64, under 6 free.

the Biosphere (page 29), La Ronde (page 96) and the Stewart Museum (page 196) and offers activities year-round.

☞ **GETTING THERE**

➤ By car, take the Jacques Cartier Bridge to Île-Ste-Hélène and follow the signs for La Ronde. Île-Notre-Dame is accessed by taking the Concorde Bridge from Cité du Havre. From downtown take the Bonaventure autoroute (Hwy. 10) south to the first exit and follow the signs for the Casino. Pay parking on site. About 10 minutes from downtown.

➤ By public transit, take the metro (yellow line) to the Île-Ste-Hélène-station.

➤ By bicycle, take the Concorde Bridge from the Cité du Havre junction and turn left.

➤ In the summer you can take a ferry from the Jacques Cartier Pier in the Old Port.

☞ **NEARBY**

➤ Biosphere, La Ronde, Stewart Museum.

☞ **COMMENT**

➤ The park offers several excellent vantage points for watching Grand Prix Formula One racing and the International Fireworks Competition (Directory of Events).

To get to these places and others in the park, including the beach, the spectacular Floralies gardens, the pool complex, playing fields, the Gilles Villeneuve Formula One race track, the Casino and the Olympic Rowing Basin, you can walk, bike or in-line skate (rentals available). Sail boards, pedal boats and canoes can also be rented. You'll find plenty of pleasant places for having a picnic and many of the sites offer stunning views of the river and city.

There's plenty going on at the park in winter too. That's when cross-country skiers, skaters and tobogganers flock to the area. Many others come during Fête des neiges (page 99), a two-week mid-winter celebration that's filled with fun activities and events.

Splish Splash
CENTENNIAL PARK

CH. MACKLE AND AV. STEPHEN-LEACOCK
(MACKLE RD. AND STEPHEN LEACOCK AVE.)
CÔTE-ST-LUC
(514) 485-6806

When you visit Centennial Park in the summer, bring your kids' bathing suits. The play area is a splash! In addition to the usual slides, swings and other playground equipment, the park has an artificial pond with pedal boats. But the biggest treat for children is the water spouts—the park's answer to a wading pool. Don't try to understand how they work, your kids will know instinctively how to make them operate. The water spouts are in the shade, so sunburns are not a concern.

☞ **SEASONS AND TIMES**
→ Year-round: Daily, dawn to dusk.

☞ **COST**
→ Free. Fees for certain activities, including the pedal boats.

☞ **GETTING THERE**
→ By car, take de Maisonneuve Blvd. west to Cavendish Blvd., turn north and continue on to Mackle Rd. (just after the Cavendish Mall). Turn west to Stephen Leacock Ave. and go north. Free parking on site. About 25 minutes from downtown.
→ By public transit, take the metro (orange line) to the Villa-Maria metro station and board the 162 bus.

☞ **NEARBY**
→ The Cavendish Mall (indoor children's play area), Côte St. Luc Public Library.

If your kids like wild animals, they'll love watching the antics of the resident groundhogs. The furry rodents live on the rocky face of the hill which becomes a very popular tobogganing site in the winter. The Côte St. Luc railway yards are a short stroll away through the woods if your kids want to see trains.

Why not take in the Canada Day festivities at the park this year? There are lots of activities for kids and families.

Room to Roam
THE LAVAL NATURE CENTRE

901 AV. DU PARC (AND BOUL. DE LA CONCORDE)
(PARK AV. AND CONCORD BLVD.)
LAVAL
(450) 662-4942

☞ **SEASONS AND TIMES**
➤ Year-round: Daily, 9 am—8 pm.

☞ **COST**
➤ Free. Charges may apply for certain activities.

☞ **GETTING THERE**
➤ By car, take Pie IX Blvd. N. across the bridge into Laval, get off at the first exit and turn west on Blvd. de la Concorde. Turn north on Ave. du Parc and look for posted signs on the right. Pay parking on site. About 30 minutes from downtown.
By public transit, take the metro (orange line) to the Henri-Bourassa station and catch the STL 72 bus. For information, call (450) 688-6520.

☞ **NEARBY**
➤ Simon Sicard hydro electric dam.

Situated in an old quarry, the Laval Nature Centre is a beautifully landscaped park that features a lake, gardens, sculptures and dramatic steep rock faces. There's lots to keep children busy, whether it's exploring the miniature pioneer farm, burning off steam at the playgrounds and playing fields, or visiting the small farm on site. They can help milk cows and feed pigs at the small farm, and see a horse, rabbits, snakes, turtles and hamsters. Nearby,

there's a small deer herd and a greenhouse with tropical plants they can visit.

In summertime the lake is popular with boaters
(rentals are available), but after it freezes, it becomes
a giant skating rink. There are also trails for cross-
country skiing and a nearby tobogganing hill offers
enthusiasts a choice of runs.

Visitors can see fossils and learn about geology
during their self-guided walk and there's even a
miniature observatory for astronomy buffs.

Down by the River
RENÉ LÉVESQUE PARK

RUE ST-PATRICK AND BOUL. LASALLE
(ST. PATRICK ST. AND LASALLE BLVD.)
LACHINE
(514) 634-3471

This neighbourhood park is a great place to go
if you want to be by the water. While you
won't find a playground or a pool, there's
still lots for kids to see and do near the river. Begin
by walking, biking or in-
line skating (rentals available) to the tip of the point
that juts into Lake St. Louis.
From there you'll have an
unobstructed view of the
water and can watch

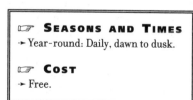

☞ **SEASONS AND TIMES**
→ Year-round: Daily, dawn to dusk.

☞ **COST**
→ Free.

ships in the St. Lawrence Seaway. Following the
two-kilometre-long path west along the waterfront
takes you past fishers who are reeling in bass and float

☞ **GETTING THERE**

→ By car, take Hwy. 20 W. to Exit 63 (Ville St. Pierre). Turn south on Gauron St. and cross the small bridge over the Lachine Canal. Turn west on St. Patrick St. and continue on until the park. Pay parking on site. About 30 minutes from downtown.

→ By public transit, take the metro (green line) to the Angrignon station and catch the 110 bus. It's a long ride.

→ By bicycle, follow the Lachine Canal bike path west, but continue going straight where the bike path turns right at the first lock.

☞ **NEARBY**

→ Fur Trade Museum, Lachine Canal bike path, Fleming Windmill.

planes taxiing on the lake. The modern sculptures that make up Lachine's Outdoor Museum are located at regular intervals. The sculptures are good places to stop for a breather and let the children run around. The path terminates at a ferry landing near the Lachine lighthouse. In the summer there is a ferry service to Old Lachine ($1 per person) and you can bring your bikes on board.

Pack a lunch for mealtime and plan on making a day of your visit. Bring plenty of liquids (there are no water fountains) and a blanket. In May and June the waterfront is inundated with swarms of non-biting shadflies.

Go Wild in the City
CAP ST. JACQUES REGIONAL PARK

20099 BOUL. GOUIN O. (GOUIN BLVD. W.)
PIERREFONDS
(514) 280-6871
WWW.CUM.QC.CA/PARCS-NATURE

Cap St. Jacques is a delightful park situated in the wildest part of the island. Dominated by maple forests and abandoned farms, the park has a sandy swimming beach, an ecological farm with animals (page 160), superb picnicking areas, restored manors and sugar shacks as well as 27 kilometres of trails for hiking and biking.

In wintertime, the trails open to the cross-country skiing crowd, and children aged 8 to 13 can take lessons. Sugaring-off parties and sleigh rides are featured in season.

The park operates an Open Air Base where up to 97 young people aged 6 to 17 can stay overnight while

☞ **SEASONS AND TIMES**
➻ Park: Year-round, daily, dawn to dusk.
Buildings: Mid-Dec—mid-Mar, mid Apr—late Oct, 10 am—5 pm (until 7 pm in summer).

☞ **COST**
➻ Free.

☞ **GETTING THERE**
➻ By car, take Hwy. 40 W. to St. Charles Blvd. Go north to Gouin Blvd., turn west and continue on until you see signs for the park. Pay parking on site ($4). About 30 minutes from downtown.
➻ By public transit, take the metro (orange line) to the Côte Vertu station and board the 64 bus. You'll have to transfer to the 68 bus (ask the driver where to get off). It's a long trip. Call the STCUM (288-6287) for more information.

☞ **NEARBY**
➻ Ecomuseum in Ste. Anne de Bellevue, Morgan Arboretum, Bois de l'Île Bizard Regional Park, Bois de Liesse Regional Park.

☞ **COMMENT**
➻ Bring mosquito repellent in late spring. Boat launching facilities.

taking ecology and outdoor courses. For more information, call 280-6778.

Delightfully Inviting
MONT ST. BRUNO PROVINCIAL PARK

330 CH. DES 25 E. (25 RD. E.)
ST. BRUNO DE MONTARVILLE
(450) 653-7544 (SUMMER ACTIVITIES)
AND (450) 653-7111 (WINTER ACTIVITIES)
WWW.SEPAQ.COM

☞ **SEASONS AND TIMES**
➤ Year-round: Daily, 8 am—sunset.

☞ **COST**
➤ Apr—Nov: Free.
Cross-country skiing (Dec—Mar):
Adults $4.50, seniors and children
$2.50, families $12.

☞ **GETTING THERE**
➤ By car, take the Jacques Cartier
Bridge to Hwy. 20 E. and follow it to
Exit 98. Turn onto Hwy. 30 S. continuing to Exit 121 and go left on
Montarville. Montarville runs into
des 25. Look for signs, the park is on
the right. Pay parking on site
($3.50). About 40 minutes from
downtown.

☞ **NEARBY**
➤ St. Bruno apple orchards.

☞ **SIMILAR ATTRACTIONS**
➤ **Mont St. Hilaire Centre
for Nature Conservation**
422 ch. des Moulins, St-Hilaire,
(450) 467-1755
www.mcgill.ca/Biology/research/msh.

Mont St. Bruno is one of the prettiest parks around Montréal. Situated on a small mountain, its luxuriant mixed deciduous forest and charming lakes demand extended exploration.

Gravel walking trails circle the park and a 40-minute hike will take you through glorious stands of beech and maple, past a lovely lake with an old water mill and into an apple orchard where the fruit is for the picking.

In the winter, there's skiing at the park, both downhill and cross-country. The slopes are patrolled and lessons are available.

Hitting the Trails
CENTRE ÉCOLOGIQUE FERNAND SÉGUIN

RTE. 132 (BEHIND L.P. PARÉ POLYVALENT SCHOOL)
CHÂTEAUGUAY
(450) 698-3123 OR (450) 698-3104

The best time to visit this Châteauguay Valley park is between fall and spring when the mosquitoes have subsided. Then you can enjoy hiking along seven kilometres of trail that lead through mature stands of deciduous trees. Signs posted along the trail identify the vegetation, which includes shag bark hickory trees and a relative of the orange tree, species that are usually found in regions farther south.

In wintertime, visitors can cross-country ski over 20 kilometres of groomed trails. Bring sunflower seeds with you as the resident chickadees and nuthatches will eat from your hands. There is a small tobogganing hill with benches and a warm-up hut. Candlelight skiing, usually offered on Saturday evenings, is a special treat.

☞ **SEASONS AND TIMES**
➤ Park: Year-round, daily, dawn to dusk. Officially closed in summer because of mosquitoes.
Buildings: Late Apr–late May, mid-Sept–late Oct, and Christmas–late Feb, daily, 10 am–5 pm.

☞ **COST**
➤ Free.

☞ **GETTING THERE**

→ By car, take Hwy. 20 W. to the Mercier Bridge and follow Rte. 132 through Châteauguay. Cross the Châteauguay River, then look for a hospital and the L. P. Paré Polyvalent School and turn left on Brisebois. The trails begin behind the school, near the arena. Free parking on site. About 35 minutes from downtown.

→ By public transit, take the metro (green line) to the Angrignon station, then take CITSO bus 14A or 14B. Get off by the hospital and L.P. Paré School (approximately 30 minutes). Cash fare $3.30. For information, call CITSO at (450) 698-3030.

☞ **NEARBY**

→ Beauharnois dam, Pointe du Buisson Archaeological Park, Canadian Railway Museum.

☞ **COMMENT**

→ Strollers can be managed on the dirt trails. French only signs, but bilingual park personnel.

Fresh Air and Fun
OKA PARK

2200 PAUL SAUVÉ
OKA
(450) 479-8337 OR 1-888-727-2652
WWW.SEPAQ.COM

Boasting woodlands, lakeshore, marshes and hills, Oka Park, located on the Lake of Two Mountains, offers outdoor enthusiasts year-round activities. In the summer, there's hiking, mountain biking, nature watching and camping (the park's turn key camping program offers full equipment rental), as well as swimming at a sandy beach.

This is a good place for viewing migrating waterfowl in the fall, and an observation tower at la Grande Baie is open to the public. However, watch out for duck hunters!

☞ **SEASONS AND TIMES**
➻ Park: Year-round, dawn to dusk, but most services only available for winter season (Dec—Mar) or camping season (May—Sept). The beach is usually open June—Sept.

☞ **COST**
➻ Free admission. Fees for some activities.

☞ **GETTING THERE**
➻ By car, take Hwy. 15 N. to Hwy. 640 W., drive past St. Eustache, then look for signs. Parking on site. About 50 minutes from downtown.
➻ By bicycle, take your bikes onto the Two Mountains train at Bois Franc or Roxboro stations and get off at Two Mountains station. A bicycle path runs past the station to the park. For information on train schedules, call STCUM at 288-6297.

The fun doesn't stop in winter. You'll find 70 kilometres of trails for cross-country skiing, ice slides and heated shelters.

Other Green Spaces

Jeanne Mance Park
AV. DU PARC AND AV. DU MONT-ROYAL
(PARK AVE. AND MOUNT ROYAL AVE.)
MONTRÉAL
(514) 872-9800

I f you have a penchant for watching people on the
go, Jeanne Mance Park is for you. Situated between
Mount Royal Park and the Plateau district, the park is
near St. Laurent Boulevard and Park Avenue, two
popular eating and shopping districts. On warm
Sunday afternoons, hundreds of people congregate at
the park near the Cartier monument to listen to the
drummers play. Going to the Tam-Tam is a summertime tradition that's worth the visit.

☞ Year-round: Daily, dawn to dusk.

☞ Free. User fees apply to some activities.

☞ Take University St. north to Av. des Pins (Pine Ave.), go
east on Pine to Park Ave. and head north. Some free parking
available on nearby streets. Minutes from downtown.
Take the metro (green line) to the Place-des-Arts station, then
board bus 80 or 129 and ride it to the park.
By bicycle, follow the Rachel Street bike path.

Lafontaine Park
RUE SHERBROOKE E. AND AV. DU PARC-LA FONTAINE
(SHERBROOKE ST. E. AND LAFONTAINE PARK AVE.)
MONTRÉAL
(514) 872-9800

T he Théâtre de Verdure stages open-air shows
for the entire family in the park during the
summer. The park boasts two lakes with pedal
boats, wading pools, cycling paths and picnicking

sites. In wintertime, you can skate on the lakes both days and evenings.

☞   Take Sherbrooke St. east to Lafontaine Park Ave.
Take the metro (orange line) to the Sherbrooke station, then walk a few blocks east.

Île de la Visitation Regional Park

2425 boul. Gouin E. (Gouin Blvd. E.)
Montréal
(514) 280-6733

You can walk or bike along five kilometres of trails and discover the park's welcome centre, miller's house and apple pressing house. Story-telling sessions in French are offered under the full moon in summer. You can fish in the reservoir behind the Simon Sicard dam. Tours of the dam are available (1-800-365-5229) and there is an observation post that's open to the public.

Fans of winter will love the small tobogganing hill located near the chalet. Cross-country ski instruction is offered to children ages 8 to 13.

☞   Park: Year-round, daily, dawn to dusk.
Buildings: Mid-Dec—mid-Mar, mid-Apr—late Oct, 10 am—5 pm (until 7 pm in summer).

☞   Free.

☞   Take Hwy. 40 E. to Papineau Ave. Go north to Gouin Blvd. and turn east. Pay parking on site. About 30 minutes from downtown.
Take the metro (orange line) to the Henri-Bourassa station, board the 48 bus and tell the driver where you're going. The closest bus stop is about three blocks from the park. Call the STCUM (288-6287) for more information.

Longueuil Regional Park

1895 RUE ADONCOUR
LONGUEUIL
(450) 646-8269

This 1,850-hectare wooded site has 25 kilometres of flat, hard-packed gravel trails for hiking and biking. That's also good news for amateur ornithologists because the forest shelters nearly 100 bird species.

The park has lots of picnic sites, but the prettiest are near the small lakes that dot the landscape. In wintertime, a few of the lakes are maintained for ice-skating. Other cold-weather activities include snowshoeing, cross-country skiing, snow boarding and tobogganing. Children's day camps are offered here.

☞   Year-round: Daily, 6 am—11 pm.

☞   Free.

☞   Take the Jacques Cartier Bridge to Longueuil and access Hwy. 132 N. Exit at Jean Paul Vincent St., turn right and look for the signs. There is a parking lot on Jean Paul Vincent. To go to the main entrance, continue to Curé Poirier E., turn right and right again on Adoncour. Parking available on site. About 35 minutes from downtown.

Take the metro (yellow line) to the Longueuil station and board STRSM bus 71. For information call (450) 463-0131.

By bicycle, take the Old Montréal-Longueuil ferry. From the Longueuil Marina, follow the bicycle path left, towards the Boucherville Islands. Take the overpass across the highway before Jean Paul Vincent and follow the signs.

Pointe aux Prairies Regional Park

12980 BOUL. GOUIN E.
MONTRÉAL
(514) 280-6691
WWW.CUM.QC.CA/PARCS-NATURE

L ocated on the island's eastern tip where the St. Lawrence River and Rivière des Prairies converge, Pointe aux Prairies Park is three parcels of land linked by trails. They constitute diverse habitats including marshes, mature forest, fields and shoreline.

The Gouin Boulevard sector, which features marshland, is a haven for waterfowl and bird watchers alike. The Sherbrooke Street sector has forests and features a popular tobogganing hill.

The park offers visitors special services including naturalist-led field tours and evening astronomy sessions, cross-country ski lessons for children ages 8 to 13, and Spring Break activities for children. Call 280-6829.

☞   Park: Year-round, daily, dawn to dusk (many facilities are closed in the winter).
Buildings: Mid-Dec—mid-Mar, and mid-Apr—late Oct, 10 am—5 pm (to 7 pm in summer).

☞   Free.

☞   Take Hwy. 40 E. to St. Jean Baptiste Blvd. Go north to Gouin Blvd. and head east. There are two entrances (14905 and 12300 Gouin Blvd.). Pay parking on site. About 30 minutes from downtown.
Take the metro (green line) to the Honoré-Beaugrand station. Board the 89 bus and transfer to the 183 bus (ask the driver to let you know where to get off).
By bicycle, use the Gouin Blvd. bicycle path for the Rivière des Prairies sectors of the park.

CHAPTER 10

HISTORICAL SITES

Introduction

Montréal has a colourful and varied heritage that's brought to life by its many museums and forts. Around the city you can listen to pipers and watch military drills at the Stewart Museum or head off the island where you can go on a tour at Fort Chambly, which was built in 1665, or head to Fort Lennox where you'll find lots of activities in the summer .

The fur trade in Québec had its own share of exciting times and you can learn about these adventures in a museum that's dedicated to the industry on which Montréal was founded. To experience daily life as an early European settler in Québec, head to the villages at Île des Moulins and Il était une fois.

For something the history books often leave out, plan an outing to the Pointe au Buisson Archaelogical Park, where the First Nations people lived and prospered 5,000 years ago. Or visit the Old Indian Village and Museum at Kahnawake and participate in a pow-wow.

Montréal is ripe with history. Get out and experience it first hand!

NOTE

Trading for Furs at THE LACHINE NATIONAL HISTORIC SITE

1255 BOUL. ST-JOSEPH (ST. JOSEPH BLVD.)
LACHINE
(514) 637-7433
WWW.PARKSCANADA.PCH.GC.CA

The amazing history of the fur trade is detailed inside this small museum, which was a fur warehouse in the 1800s. You'll learn how Scottish merchants and French Canadian voyageurs collaborated and helped Montréal dominate the fur trade. You'll also discover the story of the voyageurs who travelled thousands of kilometres by canoe to collect the furs.

☞ **SEASONS AND TIMES**
➤ Regular: Apr 1—Oct 12, daily, 10 am—12:30 pm and 1 pm—6 pm (closed Monday morning).
Fall: Oct 15—Nov 30, Wed—Sun, 9:30 am—12:30 pm and 1 pm—5 pm.

☞ **COST**
➤ Adults $2.50, seniors $2, children $1.50, under 6 free, families $6.50.

☞ **GETTING THERE**
➤ By car, take Hwy. 20 W. Exit at 32nd Ave. and go south until Victoria St. Turn east and continue on until 10th Ave. and turn south to St. Joseph Blvd., then turn west. The museum is on the left. Free parking on site. About 20 minutes from downtown.
➤ By public transit, take the metro (green line) to the Angrignon station, board the 195 bus and take it to 12th Ave.
➤ By bicycle, follow the Lachine Canal bike path west and continue along the Lake St. Louis bike path.

> ☞ **NEARBY**
> ➤ René Lévesque Park, Lachine Canal bike path.
>
> ☞ **COMMENT**
> ➤Convenience stores, restaurant, and water craft rental in proximity. Plan a 1-hour visit.

The museum's displays are primarily narrative. However some, such as a map that illustrates the voyageurs' routes, are interactive. Children can feel and smell animal pelts and attend weekend afternoon animation sessions, which are offered in the summer.

A Stroll through Yesteryear
ÎLE DES MOULINS
(Water Mill Island)

BOUL. DES BRAVES (DES BRAVES BLVD.)
TERREBONNE
(450) 471-0619

Among the most scenic parks around Montréal, Île des Moulins is a wonderful place for a family outing. The picturesque setting combines 19th century architecture with the natural beauty of the Rivière des Prairies, which meanders between tree-covered islands.

> ☞ **SEASONS AND TIMES**
> ➤ Year-round: Daily, 7 am—11 pm. Tours: afternoons and evenings. Many seasonal activities offered, call for information.
>
> ☞ **COST**
> ➤ Free.
> Theatre: Adults $10, children under 12 free.

Stroll along the asphalt trails that lead throughout the community. You'll see a flour mill, a carding mill, a seigneurial bureau, a bakery and other buildings.

The Terrebonne munici-
pal library is located in the
old sawmill that straddles
a stream.

Guided tours are led
by an actor in period costume who will explain
each building's history to
you. Historical theatre and
nature interpretation are
also offered. Bring your bikes. A bike path, a playground and an ice-cream stand are all nearby.

In wintertime, the site becomes a wonderland for
ice-skating and is the home of a winter carnival. Many
other seasonal activities are offered. Call for information.

> ☞ **GETTING THERE**
> → By car, take Pie IX Blvd. N. (it
> becomes Hwy. 25 N.) to Exit 22 E.
> Follow des Seigneurs Blvd., and turn
> right on St. Louis. Turn right on des
> Braves. Free parking on site. About
> 40 minutes from downtown.
>
> ☞ **COMMENT**
> → Plan a two-hour visit.

Early Waterways
CÔTEAU DU LAC
NATIONAL HISTORIC
SITE

308-A CH. DU FLEUVE (RIVER RD.)
CÔTEAU DU LAC (NEAR VALLEYFIELD)
(450) 763-5631
HTTP://PARCSCANADA.RISQ.QC.CA/COTEAU/EN/INDEX.HTML

Y ou can go on a guided tour of the first lock
canal built in North America. Côteau du Lac
was constructed by the British in 1779-80 to
allow troop-carrying boats to by-pass the Côteau
Rapids in the St. Lawrence River. You can also see

remnants of the French-constructed Rigolet canal at the site, which predates the British-built lock by about 30 years.

The canal was fortified to protect the lock from American attacks during the War of 1812 and several big cannons and the old blockhouse can be visited. And don't miss the model of the site that's on display at the interpretation centre. Little kids who become impatient with the visit might enjoy looking for frogs in the canal. Or, take them for ice-cream at the park nearby, or indulge in a meal at the gourmet restaurant that's housed in a former flour mill. Bring your bikes. The roads are flat and lightly travelled.

Remembering the Past
THE MONTRÉAL HOLOCAUST MEMORIAL CENTRE

5151 CH. DE LA CÔTE STE-CATHERINE
(CÔTE ST. CATHERINE RD.)
MONTRÉAL
(514) 345-2605

T he Holocaust Museum has an ugly but important theme—racism. Only by remembering our past can we hope to change the future.

Rather than dwelling on grim statistics, the bilingual displays in this museum show the lives of individual Jews in Europe prior to and during World War II. There are artifacts of family life, including children's books, a bar mitzvah invitation and a wedding contract from 1740. You'll see photos of Anne Frank, keeper of the famous diary, and pictures of community life in the Polish ghettos. The displays tend to be very positive and directed towards youth, with the emphasis on preventing a similar event from occurring.

The museum's staff and volunteers will lead

☞ **SEASONS AND TIMES**
→ Summer: Mon—Fri, 10 am—4 pm.
Regular: Sun—Thu, 10 am to 4 pm.
Reservations necessary for groups of five or more.

☞ **COST**
→ Free. Donations accepted.

☞ **GETTING THERE**
→ By car, take Hwy. 15. N. (Décarie Blvd.) to Côte Ste. Catherine and go east. Street parking available.
→ By public transit, take the metro (orange line) to the Côte Ste-Catherine station. It's a short walk west from there.

☞ **NEARBY**
→ Jewish Public Library

☞ **COMMENT**
→ Plan a 30-minute visit.

groups on tours of the museum and introduce visitors to Holocaust survivors. While the subject matter is shocking and may not be suitable for younger children, the museum claims no child has ever left the site upset. School groups can arrange to have a speaker come to the school and prepare the students for their visit. Post-visit discussions can also be arranged.

Making Crafts at
THE MUSÉE D'ART
DE ST. LAURENT
(St. Laurent Art Museum)

615 AV. STE-CROIX (ST. CROIX AVE.)
ST-LAURENT
(514) 747-7367
WWW.VILLE.SAINT-LAURENT.QC.CA

This museum has many artifacts that trace the history of European settlement of Québec. Looms, pitchforks, furniture and crosses are all found in this rich collection. An informal, guided tour will help bring the artifacts to life.

On Sundays at 2 pm, arts and crafts workshops are offered for children 4 to 12. The sessions are bilingual and no reservations are required, however arrive early to make sure you get a place.

School groups from kindergarten to high school are welcome to visit and

☞ **SEASONS AND TIMES**
➤ Year-round: Wed—Sun, noon—5 pm.

☞ **COST**
➤ Adults $3, seniors and students $2, under 6 free, families $6. Free on Wednesdays.

> ☞ **GETTING THERE**
> ➤ By car, take Hwy. 15 N. (Décarie Expressway), continuing north on
> Décarie Blvd. at the intersection of Hwy. 40. Turn east onto du College St.
> and continue to Ste. Croix Ave. Free parking on site. About 20 minutes
> from downtown.
> Take the metro (orange line) to the du College station and walk east three
> blocks to the museum.
>
> ☞ **COMMENT**
> ➤ Plan a 2-hour visit.

participate in seasonal and age-appropriate exploration workshops. Included are such activities as cooking
up an old-fashioned remedy for colds and the flu,
observing a crèche scene and lace-making. Reservations are required.

Island Fortress
FORT LENNOX
NATIONAL HISTORIC
SITE

1 AV. 62IÈME
ST. PAUL DE L'ÎLE AUX NOIX (NEAR NAPIERVILLE)
(450) 291-5700
WWW.PARKSCANADA.PCH.GC.CA

Your visit to Fort Lennox begins with a short
ferry ride that takes you to the tiny, picturesque Île aux Noix (Nut Island) in the
Richelieu River where the fort is located. The island
was strategically important during the 18th and 19th
centuries, consquently it frequently changed hands
between the French, the English and the Americans.

☞ **SEASONS AND TIMES**

→ Spring: Mid-May—late June, daily, 10 am—5 pm (weekends until 6 pm).
Summer: Late June—Labour Day, daily, 10 am—6 pm.
Fall: Labour Day—Thanksgiving, Sat—Sun, 10 am—6 pm.

☞ **COST**

→ Adults $5, seniors $3.75, children $2.50, under 6 free. Includes ferry.

☞ **GETTING THERE**

→ By car, take the Champlain Bridge to Hwy. 15 S. and take Exit 6. Follow Rte. 202 E. to the Richelieu River and turn north. After about 10 kilometres, look for signs on the river side. Free parking on site. About one hour from downtown.
→ A pedestrian ferry crosses every 30 minutes.

☞ **COMMENT**

→ Telephones can be found at the ferry dock on the mainland.

The fort, restored to look as it did during its British occupation, has displays about the soldiers' lives in those times and you can learn about the region's military history. Guided tours are offered.

The picnic area has a large field where children can run or they can hunt for snapping turtles and frogs in the fort's moat. At the games counter you can borrow Frisbees™, balls and other recreational equipment.

The fort has many activities in the summer, including Canada Day celebrations, kite flying festivals, archaeological digs and military exercises. Call for a complete schedule of events.

First Nations History
OLD INDIAN VILLAGE & MUSEUM

KAHNAWAKE, OLD MALONE HIGHWAY
(450) 638-9289 OR 638-6521

K ahnawake, which means "on the water," is the closest Mohawk settlement to Montréal and where you'll find the Old Indian Village. Surrounded by a fierce-looking palisade of sharpened logs, the grounds feature a birchbark long-house, the traditional housing for the Mohawk nation, and a teepee, used by Indian nations farther west. Also on site is a museum that has displays of First Nations' artifacts, some of which date back several centuries. Among the items you'll see are a turtle drum, bow and arrows and wampum (money made from shells). Oil paintings on the ceiling depict Kahnawake's history.

> ☞ **SEASONS AND TIMES**
> ➤ July–Labour Day, Fri–Sun, noon–5 pm. Call to confirm.
>
> ☞ **COST**
> ➤ Adults $5, seniors and children $2.
>
> ☞ **GETTING THERE**
> ➤ By car, take Hwy. 20 W. to Exit 64 and cross the Mercier Bridge, following Rte. 138 W. At the traffic circle follow signs into Kahnawake and look for signs for the museum on your right. Free parking on site and on street. About 15 minutes from downtown.

The best time for children's visits is in early July when there are special events. You can attend the totem pole-raising ceremony, taste authentic Native cuisine, join a powwow and try traditional dancing. The Three Sisters Harvest Festival is held in early October. Call for exact dates and times.

Days of Yore
IL ÉTAIT UNE FOIS . . .
UNE PETITE COLONIE

2500 RTE. 219
ACADIE
(450) 347-9756

Y ou can stroll through this historic village and experience pioneering life as it was in Québec from 1800 to 1930. About a dozen authentic buildings form the colony and are open for your inspection. Included are homes, the school house, work sheds and the blacksmith's shop. Even the toilets are circa 1850 outhouses.

Every day, villagers perform farm chores as they were done 200 years ago. If you arrive early enough in the morning, you can sample warm bread straight from the outdoor oven. With prior arrangements, you can dine on pioneer cuisine. Children will enjoy visiting the farm where they'll learn how to call turkeys and help gather eggs.

Guided tours that last about an hour are provided in French or English and can be adapted for small children.

☞ **SEASONS AND TIMES**
➤ Late June—Labour Day, Thu—Sun, 10 am—5 pm (call first).
Group visits May—Oct.

☞ **COST**
➤ Adult $5, children (2 to 12) $2, under 2 free.

☞ **GETTING THERE**
➤ By car, take Hwy. 15 S. to Exit 21, turn east and follow the signs for Napierville. In Napierville, turn north on Rte. 219. Free parking on site. About one hour from downtown.

☞ **NEARBY**
➤ René Bertrand Agricultural Museum.

☞ **COMMENT**
➤ The site is partially wheelchair accessible.

Uncovering the Past
POINTE DU BUISSON ARCHAEOLOGICAL PARK

333 EMOND
MELOCHEVILLE
(450) 429-7857

Anyone who is curious about archaeology should visit Pointe du Buisson. The park, which sits on a little peninsula in the St. Lawrence River west of Beauharnois, is considered one of the richest pre-Columbian archaeological sites in the North East.

Visit the park and learn about the First Nations people who lived and fished here 5,000 years ago.

There are several buildings at the park, including an interpretation centre, a museum and a laboratory, with exhibits that document the summer fishing camps and the people who built them. Marvel

☞ **SEASONS AND TIMES**
➤ Mid-May—Labour Day: Mon—Fri, 10 am—5 pm; weekends, 10 am—6 pm. Labour Day—mid-October: weekends, noon—5 pm.

☞ **COST**
➤ Adults $4, seniors $3, children (6 to 17) $2, under 6 free.

☞ **GETTING THERE**
➤ By car, take Hwy. 20 W. across the Mercier Bridge and follow Rte. 132 W. towards Beauharnois. The park is about three kilometres past the Beauharnois canal tunnel. Look for the blue and white signs. Free parking on site. About 50 minutes from downtown.
➤ By public transit, take the metro (green line) to the Angrignon station and catch a CITSO bus—call (450) 698-3030.

☞ **COMMENT**
➤ Groups are welcome, but telephone ahead. The site is best suited for school groups.

☞ **NEARBY**
➤ Beauharnois hydro-electric dam, St. Timothée Beach.

at an ancient dugout canoe and examine displays of cutting edges and tools.

You can visit the dig and watch the archaeologists at work. With prior arrangement, you can even help them.

The park has nature trails, but don't forget to bring insect repellent. The mosquitoes can be fierce.

The Piper's Calling
STEWART MUSEUM
AT THE FORT

ÎLE STE. HÉLÈNE
MONTRÉAL
(514) 861-6701
WWW.STEWART-MUSEUM.ORG

I t's easy to believe that you've travelled back to the 18th century while at the Fort on Île Ste. Hélène. Begin your journey at the Stewart Museum where 400 years of exploration and development in the New World are chronicled in the museum's collection of old maps, navigational equipment, scientific instruments, firearms and First Nations artifacts.

Afterward, step outside and listen to the pipers as the 78th Fraser Highlanders parade through the fort's courtyard. Next, the

---

☞ **SEASONS AND TIMES**
➤ Summer: Late May—early Sept, daily, 10 am—6 pm.
Regular: Sept—Apr, Wed—Mon, 10 am—5 pm.

☞ **COST**
➤ Adults $6, seniors and students $4, under 7 free, families $12.

Compagnie franche de la Marine will perform military drills as they did over 200 years ago.

School visits are centred on themes such as the costumes, customs and hygiene; foods and culinary traditions of the 18th century; and old-fashioned curling. Birthday parties are also available.

Plan to make a day of your visit. Near the fort, discover wooded paths and picnic areas offering magnificent views of the St. Lawrence River and the city.

☞ **GETTING THERE**

➤ By car, take the Jacques Cartier Bridge to Parc des Îles. Exit onto Île Ste. Hélène and follow the signs for La Ronde, then look for signs for the museum. Free parking (but deposit required) on site P7. About 15 minutes from downtown.

➤ By public transit, take the metro (yellow line) to the Île-Ste-Hélène station. Note that the 169 bus provides seasonal service from the Papineau metro station.

➤ By bicycle, take the Concorde Bridge from Old Montréal/Habitat 67. See also Old Montréal-Longueuil ferry (page 210).

☞ **NEARBY**

➤ La Ronde, Parc des Îles, Biosphere, Île Ste. Hélène pool.

☞ **COMMENT**

➤ Many stairs. Plan a half-day visit.

Other Historical Sites

Le Château Ramezay National Historic Site

280 RUE NOTRE-DAME E. (NOTRE DAME ST. E.)
OLD MONTRÉAL
(514) 861-3708
WWW.CHATEAURAMEZAY.QC.CA
CHAMP-DE-MARS METRO

B uilt in 1705 for Claude de Ramezay, Governor of Montréal, Le Chateau Ramezay has served as a court house, the residence of Governors General of British North America and the seat of the Government of Lower Canada. Today, the building features a collection of artifacts detailing the history of Montréal and the Province of Québec, including the first car ever driven in Montréal.

Sunday afternoon family workshops are offered in English during the school year and family tours in French are also available. Call 861-7182 at least one day in advance to reserve. School workshops (mostly in English) for grades 4 through 6 are offered on site. Call 861-3708 to reserve.

☞ Summer: June 2–Sept 29, daily, 10 am–6 pm.
Winter: Oct–May, Tue–Sun, 10 am–4:30 pm.

☞ Family workshops and tours: $12 per family.
Family, student, and group rates.

Sir George Étienne Cartier House National Historic Site

458 RUE NOTRE-DAME E. (NOTRE DAME ST. E.)
OLD MONTRÉAL
(514) 283-2282
WWW.PARKSCANADA.PCH.GC.CA
CHAMP-DE-MARS METRO

P olitician Sir George Étienne Cartier was one of the Fathers of Confederation. Visit the home where Cartier lived between 1848 and 1871. His career accomplishments are highlighted in the "East" house. Visit his elegant Victorian residence in the "West" house. Group visits can be arranged, call 283-2282.

☞ Summer: Early June–Aug 30, daily, 10 am–6 pm.
Regular: Sept–May, Wed–Sun, 10 am–noon, 1 pm–5 pm.

☞ Adults $3.50, seniors $2.80, children $1.75, under 6 free.
$1 more for theatrical performances.

Sir Wilfrid Laurier National Historic Site

205 AV. 12TH, VILLE DES LAURENTIDES (12TH AVE.)
(450) 439-3702
WWW.PARKSCANADA.PCH.GC.CA

S ir Wilfrid Laurier was the first French Canadian Prime Minister of Canada and his family home, now a historical site, has been restored and furnished as it was in the middle of the 19th century. Displays at the interpretation centre near the house depict the life and works of this great man.

Tour guides will adapt the visit for younger children, and those as young as five will be impressed with many little details that reveal how hard life was in Laurier's time. Musical Sundays, held during July and August, are probably the best time to visit. There is wheelchair access to the interpretation centre, but not to all of Laurier house.

☞ Mid-May—late June, Mon—Fri, 9 am—5 pm.
Late June—Late Aug, Wed—Sun, 10 am—6 pm.

☞ Adults $2.50, seniors $1.75, youths $1.25, under 6 free.

☞ By car, take Hwy. 15 N. to Exit 39 and follow Rte. 158 north-west until Ville des Laurentides, then begin looking for signs.
Free parking on site. About 45 minutes from Montréal Island.

Maison Saint-Gabriel

2146 PLACE DUBLIN (DUBLIN PLACE)
MONTRÉAL
(514) 935-8136
WWW.MAISONSAINT-GABRIEL.QC.CA

This farm house, which is one of the finest examples of 17th century architecture on Montréal Island, lodged the King's Wards, the women who left France for Montréal to find husbands among the Québec pioneers. Regular visits may be too dry for

☞ Summer: Late June—Labour Day, daily, 10 am—5 pm.
Regular: Mid-Feb—Late June, Labour Day—mid-Dec, Tue—Fri, 1:30, 2:30 and 3:30 pm. Guided tours only.

☞ Adults $5, seniors $4, students $3, children (6 to 12) $2, under 6 free, families $10.
Free on Saturdays in the summer from 11 am to 1 pm.

☞ By car, take Atwater St. south to Lionel Groulx and go east. Turn south on Charlevoix St., east on Wellington St., south on Du Parc-M.-Bourgeoys, and east onto Favard St. Parking on site. About 10 minutes from downtown.
By public transit, take the metro (green line) to the de l'Église station, and take bus 61 east to Dublin St. You'll have a five-minute walk.

kids, so take them to one of the special events that are held throughout the year, such as a "weekend on a farm with animals" and the feast of St. Catherine, or when there's storytelling and music. Call for a schedule. School visits are offered (935-8136) and can include such activities as a treasure hunt, experiments with medicinal plants or looking at artifacts.

Châteauguay Battle National Historic Site

2371 RIVIÈRE CHÂTEAUGUAY NORD (CHÂTEAUGUAY RIVER NORTH)
HOWICK
(450) 829-2003
WWW.PARKSCANADA.PCH.GC.CA

If American soldiers had won the Battle of the Châteauguay in 1813, Montréal might be an American city today. You can study this historic battlefield from the observation post as your guide tells you how 300 Canadian soldiers, led by Commander Charles Michel de Salaberry, defeated an army of 4,000 Americans during the War of 1812. There's a film about the battle and exhibits that illustrate the soldiers' difficult living conditions, as well as a striking gun and sword collection. Children will enjoy wearing the period uniforms that are loaned to them during their visit. Primarily narrative.

☞ Summer: Mid-May—Labour Day, Wed—Sun, 10 am—5 pm. Fall: Late Sept—late Oct, Sat—Sun, 10 am—5 pm.

☞ Adults $3.25, seniors $2.50, students $1.75, under 6 free.

☞ By car, take Hwy. 20 W. and cross the Mercier Bridge and follow Rte. 138 W. through Châteauguay towards Huntingdon. After passing Howick, look for signs. You'll cross a bridge and turn left. The site is on the left. Free parking. About 55 minutes from downtown.

Fort Chambly National Historic Site

2 RUE RICHELIEU (RICHELIEU RD.)
CHAMBLY
(450) 658-1585
WWW.PARKSCANADA.PCH.GC.CA

F ort Chambly was built in 1709 to guard the vital
portage near the rapids on the Richelieu River.
During your tour you'll learn about the original wood-
en fort that was built here in 1665 by Jacques de
Chambly and about its occupation by British and later
American armies.

Don't miss the summertime military manoeuvres. The highlight comes when actors, dressed as
18th century French soldiers, fire their long muskets.
The roar of the accompanying cannons makes quite a
sound. The Chambly Canal bicycle path and the
Chambly Lock are nearby.

☞ Summer: Mid-May—Thanksgiving, daily, 10 am—6 pm.
Spring and Fall: Mar—mid-May, mid-Oct—late Nov, Wed—Sun,
10 am—5 pm.

☞ Adults $3.75, seniors $3, children $2, under 6 free, families
$7.25.

☞ By car, take the Champlain Bridge and follow Hwy. 10 E.
towards Sherbrooke. Take Exit 22 north towards Chambly and
look for the signs. Free parking on site. About 50 minutes from
downtown.
By public transit, contact CIT Chambly-Richelieu-Carrignan
(450-658-1168) for information.

CHAPTER 11

GETTING THERE IS HALF THE FUN

Introduction

I n the case of some family outings, the journey *is* the destination. In other words, the adventure starts from the moment you set foot outdoors and the act of boating, walking, cycling, skating or travelling by train is a large part of what makes the day enjoyable for you and your kids. If you like to cycle, in-line skate or go for long walks, head to one of Montréal's popular cycling pathways—a network of scenic routes that offer the opportunity to take many interesting side trips along the way. If your kids love boats, ride the waves to Boucherville on a ferry. Or, hop aboard a double-decker train to Rigaud or Blainville. This chapter includes other interesting ways to travel, such as driving over an ice bridge and going on a bus tour. You'll even learn where children can register for a program on vehicle safety. There's also information about Montréal's transportation system. After all, a visit to Montréal isn't complete without a ride on the metro, a fun and easy way to get around the city. So check your energy levels and then rev up for a day of non-stop fun.

Lead Your Own Bike Tour
CYCLING PATHS IN MONTRÉAL

There are many paths to choose from around Montréal, whether you enjoy cycling, in-line skating, walking or jogging. Several routes on the island are popular with Montréalers, such as Angrignon Park, the Aquaduct Canal, Gouin Boulevard and the Old Port. Paths in Montréal are open between April 15 and November 1 and most have toilets and picnic areas along the way. Vélo Québec (521-8356) has maps and guidebooks of bicycle routes in the city and can help you plan a bicycling trip off the island as well. Some of the most scenic routes around Montréal are described below. Whichever path you decide to take, be sure to bring water, sunscreen, snacks, a bicycle repair kit and a first aid kit. Then, strap on your helmets and start pedalling

Lachine Canal Bicycle Path
(Montréal to Lachine)

711 BOUL. ST-JOSEPH (ST. JOSEPH BLVD.)
LACHINE
(514) 283-6054
WWW.PARKSCANADA.GC.CA/CANALLACHINE/

This 13-kilometre bike path follows the historic Lachine Canal from the Old Port to Lachine. Picnic tables and toilets are located in convenient spots along the way, so pack a lunch and spend an afternoon out on the trail. Parks Canada offers a free 90-minute tour of the canal on summer week-ends (meet at McGill Street and de la Commune Street). There's an English tour at 10:30 am and another at 2 pm in French.

☞ June—Labour Day, daily, dawn—dusk.

☞ To access the Lachine Canal bike path, drive south on Beaver Hall Hill from René Lévesque Blvd. (Beaver Hall Hill becomes McGill St.) until de la Commune St. Look for parking and then follow the signs for the entrance to the path. Call Vélo Québec for other entry points along the canal.

Parc Linéaire

300 LONGPRÉ 100
ST-JÉRÔME
(450) 436-8532

Over 200 kilometres in length, Parc Linéaire has one of the longest bike paths in North America, linking St. Jérôme to Mont Laurier. Trained personnel patrol the path in summer in case of injury or mechanical difficulties, and there are snack bars along the way, but no toilets. Parc Linéaire also offers in-season cross-country skiing on a groomed trail.

☞ Bike path: Late Apr to first snow fall. Ski trail: Dec—Mar.

☞ $10 bicycle sticker, $5 per day for a ski pass.

☞ Take Hwy. 15 N. to Exit 57. Go south on Rte. 117 and continue on to Prévost. In Prévost, turn east at the first traffic light and continue to the park. Call (514) 842-2281 for bus information.

Chambly Canal Bicycle Path

1840 BOURGOGNE
CHAMBLY
(450) 658-0681

This path runs for nearly 20 kilometres along the Chambly Canal linking Chambly and St. Jean sur Richelieu. In St. Jean, the path meets the Estriade and Montérégie bike paths and there is an information centre with an exhibition about the canal that is open to the public. The site has toilets and picnic tables.

☞ Year-round: Daily.

☞ Take Hwy. 10 E. to Exit 22. Turn north towards Chambly, then east on Bourgogne. For bus information, call CIT Chambly-Richelieu-Carrignan at (450) 658-1168.

For something a little different, why not try biking across a bridge or along a dike? The following routes offer bikers, in-line skaters and hikers a little something out of the ordinary to do on a sunny day.

Ice Breaker Bridge

ÎLE DES SOEURS (NUN'S ISLAND)
(514) 872-6093

The world's longest bridge used exclusively by cyclists, in-line skaters and pedestrians spans the St. Lawrence River. Originally designed to protect the Champlain Bridge from ice floes, the Ice

☞ Victoria Day–Thanksgiving: Daily, 7 am–10 pm.

☞ Take Hwy. 15 S. to Île des Soeurs and turn left onto René Lévesque Blvd. The bridge access is next to the fire station. For bike directions, call Vélo Québec.

Breaker Bridge's two-kilometre trail offers spectacular views of the cityscape and the St. Lawrence River. The bridge path meets three other cycling trails that lead to Ste. Catherine, St. Lambert and Île Notre Dame.

Maritime Seaway Dike

T he Seaway Dike is a wide, flat, paved road reserved for cyclists, in-line skaters and hikers. Stretching from Kahnawake to the Montréal Casino, it provides access to many fun sites that are covered elsewhere in this guide, such as the Canadian Railway Museum (page 57), The Ecomuseum at St. Constant (page 63) and the beach and campsite at Ste. Catherine Park (page 107). Keep your eyes peeled for the tasty wild strawberries that grow on the dike's slopes. Bring a picnic and have lunch at Île Notre Dame or Île des Soeurs, which you pass along the way.

☞ Apr—Oct: Daily, dawn—10 pm.

☞ The dike can be accessed from the Ice Breaker Bridge, Île Notre Dame, the St. Lambert locks and the Ste. Catherine locks.

Ahoy Matey!
TRAVEL BY BOAT

I f your kids love the water, why not take them for a trip on one of Montréal's ferry boats? It's an inexpensive and easy way to entertain youngsters. Looking for something a little more exciting? Then sign up for a day of jet boating, or run the rapids on a raft. You can even tour around the Old Port on the Amphibus (a vehicle that can travel on land and in the water). You'll also find a listing for boat cruises in this section. So round up the crew and set sail for some watery fun.

Bellerive-Île Charron Ferry Boat

RUE MERCIER AND RUE BELLERIVE (MERCIER ST. AND BELLERIVE ST.)
MONTRÉAL
(514) 281-8000

This ferry runs between Montréal and the Boucherville Islands, an area that's popular with cyclists, naturalists and families on an outing for the day. There is a regional park with bike paths, wooden bridges, wetlands that are teeming with waterfowl, a golf course and a restaurant. Kayak, canoe, pedal boat and bicycle rentals are available.

☞ By car, take Sherbrooke St. E. until des Ormeaux St. and turn south. Then turn west on Bellerive St. The ferry leaves from the foot of Mercier St. and Bellerive.

☞ By public transit, take the metro (green line) to the Honoré-Beaugrand station, then catch the 185 bus.

☞ By bicycle, use the Notre Dame bike path, or ride along Sherbrooke St.

Longueuil-Old Montréal Ferry Boat

RUE DE LA COMMUNE AND QUAI JACQUES-CARTIER
(DE LA COMMUNE ST. AND JACQUES CARTIER PIER)
OLD MONTRÉAL
(514) 281-8000

This pedestrian ferry, which links Montréal to the South Shore and Île Ste. Hélène, offers great views of the city and of ships in the harbour. It is possible to make several loops with this ferry, returning from Longueuil to Montréal via the Boucherville Islands (two other ferries are involved), or via the St. Lambert locks, and either Parc des Îles or the Ice Breaker Bridge.

There is no extra charge for bringing bikes on the ferry. There is a snack machine but no toilets or phones on board.

☞ Summer: Late June—early Sept, daily, 11 am—6 pm.
Other times: May—late June and early Sept—early Oct, Sat—Sun, 11 am—6 pm.

☞ Bellerive-Île Charron Ferry: $3.25 per person.
Longueuil-Montréal Ferry: $3.50 per person (Montréal-Longueuil); $3 per person (Montréal-Île- Ste. Hélène) $2.75 per person (Parc des Îles-Île Charron).

☞ By car, take Beaver Hall Hill (it becomes McGill St.) south to de la Commune St. and then go east a few blocks. Pay or metered parking. The club meets beside the river behind a large hangar. Minutes from downtown.
By public transit, take the metro (orange line) to the Champ-de-Mars station. Walk south on Gosford St.

These other boating adventures are also available in the Montréal area:

AMPHIBUS TOUR

BOUL. ST-LAURENT AND RUE DE LA COMMUNE
(ST. LAURENT BLVD. AND DE LA COMMUNE ST.)
(514) 849-5181
WWW.AMPHIBUSTOUR.QC.CA

BATEAU-MOUCHE

QUAI JACQUES-CARTIER (JACQUES CARTIER PIER)
(514) 849-9952
WWW.BATEAU-MOUCHE.COM

CROISIÈRES DU PORT DE MONTRÉAL (MONTRÉAL PORT CRUISES)

BASSIN DE L'HORLOGE (CLOCK TOWER BASIN)
(514) 842-9300, 842-3871 (RESERVATIONS).

CROISIÈRES NOUVELLE-ORLÉANS (NEW ORLEANS CRUISES)

QUAI JACQUES-CARTIER (JACQUES CARTIER PIER)
(514) 842-9300, 842-3871 (RESERVATIONS).

JET ST-LAURENT

QUAI JACQUES-CARTIER (JACQUES CARTIER PIER)
(514) 284-9607

SAUTE MOUTONS (JET BOATING)

BASSIN DE L'HORLOGE (CLOCK TOWER BASIN)
(514) 284-9607

Going Public
CITY BUSES
AND THE METRO

STCUM (Société de transport de la Communauté urbain de Montréal)
(514) 288-6287 (routes and schedules)
WWW.STCUM.QC.CA

The Metro

The Montréal metro system currently has 65 stations located on four lines that are colour-coded
blue, green, orange and yellow. To get to your destination, refer to the metro system map that's posted
inside each station. Locate the stop you want, note the
colour of the metro line and the name of the terminus
in the direction you are heading. For example, if you
are downtown and your destination is the Biodome
(metro stop Pie IX), head east by taking the green line
in the direction of Honoré-Beaugrand.

The customer service office, located at the Berri-
UQAM metro station, offers the following publica-
tions: planibus (bus schedules), network map, metro
guide and commuter train schedules. Maps of the
metro are also available at each station.

☞ **COMMENT**
➤ Bikes can be carried on the metro by those over 16 years of age, or accompanied by an adult, between 10 am and 3 pm and after 7 pm (weekdays). On
Saturday, Sunday and holidays, bikes can be transported all day on the metro
but individuals can only board the front car of the train with their bicycles
(maximum of four bikes).

The Bus System

T he STCUM has 151 bus lines that it operates regularly in Montréal and other communities on the island. Buses require exact change, tickets or monthly passes.

☞ **SEASONS AND TIMES**
➤ Year-round: Daily.
Metro: Open at 5:30 am. Closing times vary depending on the line; between 11 pm and 12:30 am (weekdays and Sundays); between 11 pm and 1 am (Saturday).
Buses: Each route varies. Bus schedules are located at each bus stop or call Télbus (the number is posted at each stop) for a recording that announces the arrival times of the next three buses at that stop. For detailed information for your location, call 288-6287. Special hours on statutory holidays.

☞ **COST**
➤ Adult Fares:
Tourist Card – $7 for 1 day, $14 for 3 days.
Single ticket – $2 · Book of tickets – 6 tickets for $8.25.
Monthly passes – $47 · Weekly passes – $12.50.

Reduced Fares (seniors and students):
Tourist Card – no reduction from adult fare. · Single tickets – $1.
Book of tickets – 6 tickets for $4.25 · Monthly passes – $20.
Weekly passes – $6.50.
Photo ID may be required for reduced rates.

Riding the Rails
COMMUTER TRAINS

(514) 288-6287 (STCUM INFORMATION)
(514) 287-2464 (AGENCE MÉTROPOLITAINE DE TRANSPORT)
WWW.AMT.QC.CA

A short trip on a commuter train is especially fun for kids if they get to sit upstairs in a double-decker car. Trains depart from downtown every

☞ **SEASONS AND TIMES**
➤ Year-round: Daily, 6 am—11 pm.
May vary.
Frequency of trains varies, so call for
the schedule.

☞ **COST**
➤ Varies depending on how many
zones you are travelling through
(there are 8 zones). TRAM passes
(monthly train passes) can be used
on buses and the metro.

☞ **COMMENT**
➤ Not wheelchair accessible. Bikes
can be transported during certain
hours on specific trains. Visit the
Web site, or call 287-2464 for
details.

day on three lines; the Two Mountains train at Central Station and the Rigaud and Blainville trains at Windsor Station.

Plan an afternoon excursion and stop off at one of the many scenic destinations along the railroad. The Two Mountains route passes Bois de Liesse Park, Bigras Island and Laval Island, ending near St. Eustache. Most trains on the Rigaud line only go as far as Dorion —however, two trains go to Rigaud daily.

The majority of commuter train stations have telephones, shelters, bus stops, car parks and bike racks. Some have bathrooms and snack bars. The trains themselves have no facilities. The best time to ride the rails is in the late morning or early afternoon, not during rush hours (6 am to 9 am, and 3:30 pm to 7 pm).

Train tickets can be purchased from machines at each station. Bus tickets are no longer accepted. Bus passes are acceptable for travel within Zone 1 (Windsor Station to Dorval). Train passes can be bought at Central, Windsor, Beaconsfield, Montréal West, Vendôme and Jean Talon stations and selected variety stores.

❤❤❤

The Wheels on the Bus Go Round and Round
BUS TOURS

Nothing beats a bus tour if you want an overview of greater Montréal. You'll get an introduction to the Old Port, Mount Royal, St. Joseph's Oratory, the Olympic Stadium and many other points of interest in the city. The following companies offer tours of Montréal with bilingual guides and brief stops along the way. Several companies offer "hop on, hop off" tickets for passengers who want to leave the tour at designated stops and spend time exploring the sights. The tickets entitle their bearers to resume the tour on a bus that passes by later in the day.

Royal Autocar

INFOTOURISTE CENTRE
1001 DU SQUARE-DORCHESTER (DORCHESTER SQUARE)
MONTRÉAL
(514) 990-7316
WWW.AUTOCARROYAL.COM

This company offers three to eight-hour bus tours of some of Montréal's finest sights. They have several double-decker buses, which are a hit with kids. They also offer package deals, "hop on, hop off" tickets and bus rentals. Some tours are only available in the summer months. Call for details.

Gray Line
1140 RUE WELLINGTON (WELLINGTON STREET)
(514) 934-1222
WWW.GRAYLINE.COM/DESTINATIONS/DESTINATION.CFM

Gray Line offers five different tours of Montréal, including combination excursions such as a bus tour and cruise of the St. Lawrence. Plan a day trip and get a package deal that includes entry fees to the Biodome, the Olympic Tower and the Botanical Gardens. The C1 tour runs year-round while others are offered between May and October. They also have tours that go to Ottawa and Quebéc City. Call for schedules and prices.

☞ Prices vary, depending on the package and the length of the tour. A one-hour tour is around $12 for adults, while a full-day tour including admission to sites is around $42.
Adults $12 to $42, seniors and students $10 to $38, children (5 to 12) $6 to $25.

La Balade bus tour

QUAI JACQUES-CARTIER (JACQUES CARTIER PIER)
(514) 283-5219

All that walking around the Old Port got you tired out? Catch a ride on La Balade, a long, open shuttle bus that runs the length of the Old Port. Commentary is provided about nearby points of interest.

☞ Daily: Late May—early Sept.

☞ Adults $3.50, seniors and students $2.50, children $1.50.

Cool!
IT'S AN ICE BRIDGE

BETWEEN HUDSON AND OKA
(450) 458-4732

I n warmer months, a ferry service operates across the Ottawa River between Hudson and Oka. But as soon as the temperature drops and the river freezes, crews begin watering the route twice daily. Once the ice has reached

> ☞ **SEASONS AND TIMES**
> → Dec—Mar, weather permitting.
>
> ☞ **COST**
> → $4.50 per car.
>
> ☞ **GETTING THERE**
> → Take Hwy. 40 W. until Exit 26 and follow signs for the ferry.

between 31 and 33 centimetres in thickness, the ice bridge is ready and is opened for automobile traffic. You may not be able to cross the river in late spring when the ice is too thin for cars, but still too thick for the ferry to pass through. On those days you will have to find an alternate route.

Safe Cycling at
VILLAGE DE SECURITÉ LASALLE
(LaSalle Safety Village)

8745 BOUL. LASALLE (LASALLE BLVD.)
LASALLE
(514) 367-4664

☞ **SEASONS AND TIMES**
➤ Year-round: Mon—Fri, 8:30 am—12 pm and 1 pm—5 pm. The centre is occasionally open on weekends, but no animation is provided.

☞ **COST**
➤ Free.

☞ **GETTING THERE**
➤ By car, take Hwy. 15 to Exit 62 and go west on de la Vérendrye. Turn south onto Shevchencko St. then east on Champlain and north onto Gagne. Free parking on site. About 15 minutes from downtown.
By public transit, take the metro (green line) to the Angrignon station, and then board bus 110.

☞ **NEARBY**
➤ Boomerang, McDonald's Playland.

☞ **COMMENT**
➤ Bring your own bikes, as the centre only has a few to lend out.

Located in the Place LaSalle parking lot, the Village de Securité LaSalle makes learning about transportation safety fun and exciting for kids ages 4 to 12. Here, kids can wheel their bikes around a miniature village, complete with paved roads, street signs and buildings. On-site animators educate children about bicycle, railway and road safety. Courses with other themes such as fire prevention, public transportation and electricity safety are also available. Group visits, which last about 90 minutes, are offered during the week.

CHAPTER 12

FARTHER AFIELD

Introduction

While this guide was designed to provide you with a variety of fun outings in the Montréal area, a few sites that are a bit farther afield couldn't be left out. At Prehistoric World in Morrisburg, your kids can come face-to-face with all their favourite dinosaurs. To see birds, travel to the Exotic Birds Zoo where they can shake hands with a parrot. Children can learn all about snowmobiles at the Bombardier Museum and learn about mining by touring the depths of the Capelton Mine. For something really different, head out with the gang to the Vermont Teddy Bear Company and see how teddy bears are made. Visit the Gilles Villeneuve Museum in Berthierville and test your skills in a Formula One racing simulator. While all these sites fall outside the guide's "one-hour rule" for travel, they're worth the extra kilometres.

Living History at
THE ODANAK INDIAN VILLAGE

108 Waban-Aki (near Pierreville)
(450) 568-2600
www.odanak.affaires-411.com

The best time for kids to visit Odanak is during the powwow, held on the first Sunday in July, when they'll experience first-hand traditional dancing, campfires, a festive parade and more. Other times you can take a guided tour of the village and sample authentic cuisine.

Odanak, which means "our home" in Abenaki, also houses the Abenaki Historical Museum, where interactive exhibits will help you learn more about the Abenaki culture. The Catholic church nearby is decorated with carvings and several boutiques sell First Nations handicrafts including tree root baskets.

The village is situated along the picturesque St. François River, and there are picnic tables where you can eat your lunch.

Seasons and Times

→ Summer: May—Oct, Mon—Fri, 10 am—5 pm; weekends, 1 pm—5 pm. Winter: Nov—Apr, Mon—Fri, 10 am—5 pm.
Reservations required for guided tours.

Cost

→ Adults $4, children (under 13) $2.

Getting There

→ By car, take the Louis Hippolyte Lafontaine Tunnel to Hwy. 20 E. following it until the junction with Hwy. 30. Take Hwy. 30 N. to Sorel (it ends there) and continue east on Hwy. 132 for about 30 kilometres. Turn left to enter Odanak immediately after crossing the St. François River bridge. Free parking on site. About 90 minutes from downtown.

Close Encounters with Dinosaurs at
PREHISTORIC WORLD

UPPER CANADA ROAD
MORRISBURG, ONTARIO
(613) 543-2503

I t's one thing to read about dinosaurs, it's quite another to see them up close in a primeval forest. Prehistoric World has faithfully reproduced 50 life-size dinosaurs and other prehistoric beasts, including a stegosaurus, a tyrannosaurus, a woolly mammoth and a triceratops.

Placed strategically along a concrete trail that winds through the park, each dinosaur is accompanied by a panel containing bilingual biographical information. The setting is incredibly authentic-looking, with ferns growing abundantly on the forest floor.

Composed of a metal frame covered with concrete and then painted, each dinosaur requires about five months to complete. You may spot some under construction. But unlike Hollywood's reproductions, these dinosaurs don't attack. In fact, they don't move. All of Prehistoric World's exhibits are stationary.

☞ **SEASONS AND TIMES**
➤ Summer: Late May—early Sept, daily, 10 am—4 pm.
Fall: Early Sept—mid-Oct, Sat—Sun, 10 am—4 pm.

☞ **COST**
➤ Adults $6, children $4.25, under 4 free.
Group rates available.

Some kids will like digging for fossils in the park's sandy palaeontology pit, while others will be content running around the adjacent field. Tables have been provided for picnicking. A nearby restaurant offers take-out.

☞ **GETTING THERE**

➺ By car, take Hwy. 40 W. (it becomes Hwy. 401). Take Exit 758 south and follow the posted signs. Free parking on site. About 90 minutes from downtown.

☞ **NEARBY**

➺ Upper Canada Village, Upper Canada Bird Sanctuary.

☞ **COMMENT**

➺ The concrete path is bumpy. Plan a 1-hour visit.

☞ **SIMILAR ATTRACTION**

➺ **Jurassic Park**
St. Leonard d'Aston (near Drummondville)
(819) 399-3466

Making Tracks to the
EXOTIC BIRDS ZOO

2699 RTE. 139
ROXTON POND
(450) 375-6118

This zoo is for the birds—more than 450 of them, representing 125 exotic species from South America, Africa and Australia. Visitors can guide themselves around the outdoor site following a one-kilometre trail. The birds are housed in cages and descriptive brochures, available at the entrance, will tell you about each one.

While they're beautiful to look at, it's the birds' personalities that appeal to kids. Some are real hams

☞ **SEASONS AND TIMES**
➤ Mid-June—mid-Sept: Daily, 10 am—5 pm. Season sometimes extended, weather permitting.

☞ **COST**
➤ Adults $6, children $4, under 6 free.
Group rates available.

☞ **GETTING THERE**
➤ By car, take Hwy. 10 E. towards Sherbrooke to Exit 68 and drive north on Rte. 139. following signs for the Granby Zoo. Continue on 139 past the Zoo, go through Roxton Pond and look for a big sign on your left marking the Exotic Bird Zoo. Free parking on site. About 75 minutes from downtown.

☞ **NEARBY**
➤ Granby Zoo.

☞ **COMMENT**
➤ The toilets here are primitive and there are no sinks. An on-site boutique sells birds, supplies and souvenirs. Plan a 1-hour visit.

and like to perform gymnastic tricks. One bird, named Elvis, sings to anyone who will listen. Others talk, speaking in English and French. Children will enjoy shaking hands with the parrots (they need to be aware that quick movements frighten the birds) and can watch chicks being hand-fed. Some of the birds can be held for photo shoots.

Better Watch Out!
SANTA'S VILLAGE

987 RUE MORIN (MORIN RD.)
VAL DAVID
1-800-287-6635
WWW.NOEL.QC.CA

S anta's summer hide-away offers kids such a variety of things to do, they won't know where to start. This outdoor theme park features more than 20 activities and attractions including baseball-pitching machines, slides, a labyrinth, a climbing wall, a tree house, go-carts, pony rides, boat rides and face-painting. There's also a petting farm where kids can get up close to goats, ducks, rabbits and geese.

In keeping with the holiday spirit, children can visit Santa's house, sit on his knee, or write letters to him which they can mail at the village post office.

The park's terrain is quite hilly. It's best to avoid visiting on weekends, as the crowds tend to overwhelm the facilities.

☞ **SEASONS AND TIMES**
➤ Summer: June–July, daily, 10 am–6 pm.
Spring and Fall: Late May and Aug–Labour Day, Sat–Sun, 10 am–6 pm.

☞ **COST**
➤ Adults and children $8.50, seniors $6.50, under 2 free.
Credit cards accepted.

☞ **GETTING THERE**
➤ By car, take Hwy. 15 N. to Exit 76 and follow the signs. Free parking on site. About 90 minutes from downtown.
➤ By bus, Limocar Laurentides services the region. The bus terminal is on the street level of the Berri-UQAM metro station. For more information, call 842-2281.

☞ **COMMENT**
➤ Partially wheelchair accessible. Plan a 3-hour visit.

Snow Day at
THE J. ARMAND BOMBARDIER MUSEUM

1001 AV. J.A. BOMBARDIER (J. A. BOMBARDIER AVE.)
VALCOURT
(450) 532-5300
WWW.FJAB.QC.CA/MUSEEJAB

D id you know that the first snowmobile was built in Québec by J. Armand Bombardier? You'll learn all about Mr. Bombardier and see the garage where he invented the snowmobile at the Bombardier Museum. Other themes presented at the museum cover science, production, commerce and there are also temporary expositions. Few of the displays are interactive, but there are films and videos to watch and youngsters can make crafts in the summer. The front desk also loans sports equipment if you wish to play games on the museum's extensive grounds.

☞ **SEASONS AND TIMES**
➤ Summer: May—Thanksgiving, daily, 10 am—5 pm (until 5:30 pm in Aug).
Winter: Oct—Apr, Tue—Sun, 10 am—5 pm.

☞ **COST**
➤ Adults $5, seniors and students $3, under 6 free.
School programs: Starting at $2 per student.

☞ **GETTING THERE**
➤ By car, take Hwy. 10 E. to Exit 90. Turn north on Rte. 243 towards Waterloo, then west on Rte. 222 and begin looking for blue highway signs to the museum. About 75 minutes from Montréal. Free parking on site.

The museum has a range of programs for schools groups where students as young as nursery school age can learn about winter clothing, attend theatre performances, make crafts, go on guided tours of the museum with employees who knew Mr Bombardier and visit the adjacent Ski-doo™ assembly plant. The length of the visits varies from 30 minutes to an entire day. School groups should reserve at least two weeks in advance, especially in April and May, and ask for animation services.

Down in the Deeps
CAPELTON MINE TOURS

800 RTE. 108
(NEAR NORTH HATLEY)
(819) 346-9545

Capelton Mine offers visitors the chance to visit a copper mine that operated in the late 1800s. The two-hour guided tour begins with visitors donning rain-coats and hardhats, then embarking on a tractor-pulled wagon ride up to the mine. As you proceed through the electrically-lit tunnels, your guide will explain 1860s mining techniques and you'll see stalactites, stalagmites and bats. There is a chapel in the mine that has amazing acoustics and is the

☞ **SEASONS AND TIMES**
➤ May–Oct, by reservation.

☞ **COST**
➤ Adults $12.95, children (6 to 15) $7.95, under 6 free.

☞ **GETTING THERE**
➤ By car, take the Champlain Bridge to Hwy. 10 E. and continue on to Exit 121. Take Hwy. 55 S. to Exit 29 and proceed on Rte. 108 to North Hatley. From North Hatley, follow the blue highway signs to the mine. Free parking on site. About 1 hour and 45 minutes from downtown.

site of periodic concerts and storytelling sessions
(primarily in French). Call for a schedule.

Be prepared to do a lot of walking—the mine is
huge. Dress warmly, and pack extra clothes. The tunnels are a chilly 9°C year-round and filled with rusty
mud. Children as young as four are welcome to walk
through the mine, but must remember not to touch
things. Younger children can be carried in a backpack
(one is available for loan). However, be careful as
some of the ceilings are low and there are steep stairs.

Outside by the visitors' centre there is a small
museum, a covered bridge and a beautiful bicycle path
along the Massawippi River extending from
Sherbrooke to North Hatley. Some bicycles and a
trailer are available for rent. Hiking trails wander
through the 260 hectares of land.

Little House on the Farm
ALMANZO WILDER HOMESTEAD

BURKE RD.
MALONE, NEW YORK
(518) 483-1207

M any Montréalers are familiar with the
Little House on the Prairie books written
by Laura Ingalls Wilder, however few may
realize that some of her stories are set only an hour
from Montréal. *Farmer Boy*, a delightful recounting
of pioneer life in upstate New York, is based on her
husband Almanzo's childhood.

The Wilder farm, which was abandoned after being struck by lightning, is being restored to look as it did in 1860. The best time to visit is during the summer when there are special events. In the past these have included Civil War re-enactments and sheep shearing. Call for a schedule. Other times, you can go on a guided tour (in English only) of the farm house and see a slide show in the barn. The tours are narrative in nature.

☞ **SEASONS AND TIMES**
→ Late May–Labour Day: Tue–Sat, 11 am–4 pm; Sun, 1–4 pm.

☞ **COST**
→ Adults $4, children $2.

☞ **GETTING THERE**
→ By car, take Hwy. 20 W. to Exit 64. Cross the Mercier Bridge and follow Rte. 138 W. to New York State, then follow NY Rte. 30 to Malone. From Malone, go east on Rte. 11 about 6 kilometres to South Burke Rd. and turn south. Look carefully for signs. About 75 minutes from Montréal. Free parking on site.

☞ **COMMENT**
→ This site has great potential, but presently is not as kid-friendly as it could be. Plan a 1-hour visit.

There's a hiking trail to the river, if anyone wants to stretch their legs after the car ride.

Racing Off to
THE GILLES
VILLENEUVE MUSEUM

960 AV. GILLES VILLENEUVE (GILLES VILLENEUVE AVE.)
BERTHIERVILLE
1-800-639-0103 OR (450) 836-2714 (LONG DISTANCE)
WWW.VILLENEUVE.COM

This museum is dedicated to the late Gilles Villeneuve, a Formula One racing car driver and Berthierville native. There are souvenirs of both Gilles' and his son Jacques' careers, including trophies, race cars and photos. The museum also features a recreated racing pit, tire barriers, steel guard rails and racing flags. You can test your driving skills aboard the Ferrari-like virtual reality racing simulator or on the slot-car race track, and view videos and films about Québec's favourite son and hero of Formula One racing.

☞ **SEASONS AND TIMES**
➤ Year-round: Daily, 9 am–4 pm.

☞ **COST**
➤ Adults $6, seniors (over 55) $5, students (6 to 18) $4, under 5 free, families (two adults and two children) $14.95.

☞ **GETTING THERE**
➤ By car, take Hwy. 40 E. towards Québec City and take Exit 144. Follow Rte. 158 south (it becomes Gilles-Villeneuve Ave. after it crosses Rte. 138).

Voyage to the Past at the VILLAGE QUÉBECOIS D'ANTAN *(Village of Yesteryear)*

1425 RUE MONTPLAISIR (MONTPLAISIR RD.)
DRUMMONDVILLE
(819) 478-1441 OR 1-877-710-0267
WWW.VILLAGEQUEBECOIS.QC.CA

This historic village recaptures the life of a rural Québec village between 1810 and 1910. There are nearly 70 buildings to visit including a general store, a bakery, a blacksmith's shop and a candle maker's shop. Actors in period costumes will guide you through the site.

Traditional Québecois cuisine, such as tourtière, pea soup and baked beans are served at the two on-site restaurants or enjoy contemporary cuisine at the cafeteria. Children can play in the labyrinth or visit the farm and feed the animals. There are special events, such as a St. Jean Baptiste parade on June 24, and an old-fashioned Christmas celebration with games in August.

☞ **SEASONS AND TIMES**
➙ June: Daily, 9:30 am—5 pm.
Jul—Aug: Daily, 10 am—6 pm.
Sept: Daily, 10 am—5 pm.

☞ **COST**
➙ Adults $15, seniors and students $13, children (under 13) $6, families $34.

☞ **GETTING THERE**
➙ Take Hwy. 20 E. to Exit 177 or 181 (Drummondville) and follow the posted signs. About 90 minutes from downtown. Parking on site.

☞ **SIMILAR ATTRACTION**
➙Upper Canada Village
County Rd. 2 , Morrisburg
1-800-437-2233 · www.parks.on.ca

Other Places that are Farther Afield

Vermont Teddy Bear Company

6655 SHELBURNE RD.
SHELBURNE, VERMONT
(802) 985-3001 EXT. 1800 (TOURS AND SPECIAL EVENTS)
WWW.VERMONTTEDDYBEAR.COM

You can learn all about the history of teddy bears and watch them being made during the half-hour tour offered at the Vermont Teddy Bear Company. But be prepared—your kids will most likely want to buy a furry friend of their very own. If you're watching your budget, let them send their friends virtual Bear-Grams from the company's Web site instead. Birthday parties that include a tour, a teddy bear and goodie bag for each guest and a Ben and Jerry's cake can be arranged. Call (802) 985-1339.

☞ Year-round, Mon—Sat, every 30 minutes, 9:30 am—4 pm; Sun, every 30 minutes, 10:30 am—4 pm.

☞ Tour: Adults $1, children (under 13) free.

☞ Take Hwy. 15 S. (it becomes I-87 at the U.S. border) to Exit 42. Take US-11 E. to US-2 and continue southeast on US-2 to VT-78 E. (towards Swanton), then take I-89 south to Exit 13 and go south on US-7 for about 9 kilometres. The factory is on US-7. About 2 hours and 30 minutes from Montréal.

Mikey's Fun Factory

1020 MONTREAL RD.
CORNWALL, ONTARIO
(613) 938-1619

M ikey's Fun Factory is a warehouse full of games. There are batting cages, pool tables, a video arcade, a minigolf course complete with a waterfall, a haunted house and a loop-the-loop tire. Birthday packages are available.

☞ Year-round: Daily, 11 am—10 pm.

☞ Minigolf: Adults $5, children (5 to 12) $4, under 5 free. Half-price on Wednesdays. All other activities are coin-operated.

☞ Take Hwy. 20 W. (it becomes the 401) to Boundary Rd. (Hwy. 44) and go south to Montreal Rd. Go west on Montreal Rd. and continue about 4 kilometres to the warehouse. Free parking on site. About 1 hour from Montréal.

12 Months of Fun
DIRECTORY OF EVENTS

JANUARY
To early March
Dog Sledding
Old Port of Montréal, Jacques-Cartier entrance
(514) 496-7678 · 1-800-971-7678
www.oldportofmontreal.com/events/winter/index.html

To mid-February
Crèches display
St. Joseph's Oratory
(514) 733-8211

Late January
Brome Winter Carnival
and Dog Sled Racing
Knowlton
(450) 242-2870

Late January to early February
Artapalooza
Saidye Bronfman Centre
(514) 739-2301 · 739-7944
www.thesaidye.org

Late January to mid-February
Fête des Neiges
Parc des Îles
(514) 872-4537

FEBRUARY
Late January to early February
Artapalooza
Saidye Bronfman Centre
(514) 739-2301 · 739-7944
www.thesaidye.org

To mid-February
Crèches display
St. Joseph's Oratory
(514) 733-8211

To mid-February
Fête des Neiges
Parc des Îles
(514) 872-4537

Late February to early March
Montréal International
Children's Film Festival
Cinéma Impérial
(514) 848-0300

Chinese Ice Sculptures
Botanical Garden
(514) 872-1400

Winter carnival
Fort Chambly
(450) 658-1585

Winter carnival
Île des Moulins
(450) 471-0619

Maple Sugar time (sugaring-off)

MARCH
Early March
Montréal International
Children's Film Festival
Cinéma Impérial
(514) 848-0300

Sunday nearest March 17
St. Patrick's Day Parade
Downtown Montréal

Mid-March
Montréal National Great
Outdoors Show
Olympic Park
(514) 327-4464

Maple Sugar time (sugaring-off)

APRIL
Early April
Spring National Postage Stamp
Show
Place Bonaventure
(514) 397-2222

Mid-April
Jeux de Montréal
5000 kids in 22 sporting events
1000 Émile-Journault
(514) 872-6911

Frog hunt
Ecomuseum
Ste. Anne de Bellevue
(514) 457-9449

MAY
Mother's Day Run
Kids' Races
Mount Royal Park
(514) 898-9476

Mid-May
Montréal Air Show
Mirabel
(514) 790-1245

Mid-late May
Museum Day
(514) 845-6873
Free admission to 25 Montréal
museums
Free shuttle bus from Centre
Infotouriste at Dorchester Square

Late May
Montréal Bike Fest
Children's Tour de l'Île de
Montréal
25 kilometre bike circuit of
Montréal
Maison des cyclistes
(514) 521-8356

Late May
Family Day
Westmount Park

(514) 989-5226

Late May to early June
Des Coups de Théâtre
(514) 499-2929
www.les400coups.com

JUNE
Late May to early June
Des Coups de Théâtre
(514) 499-2929
www.les400coups.com

Early June
Ormstown Fair
(450) 829-2776
www.ormstownfair.com

June
Benson & Hedges International
fireworks competition
La Ronde · Île Ste-Hélène metro
(514) 872-4537

Mid-June
From Ice and Water
Downtown Montréal
Celebration of Northern Cultures
(514) 521-2714

Mid-June
Montréal Fringe Festival
McGill University
(514) 849-3378

Mid-June
Worldwide Kite Rendez-Vous
Arthur Therrien Park
(514) 765-7213
www.total.net/~rvmcv

June 21
National Aboriginal Day
(514) 278-4040

June 23-24
Fête Nationale
(514) 849-2560

Late June
Carifiesta
Downtown · Place-des-Arts Metro
(514) 735-2232

Late June
Intercultural Festival
Laval Nature Centre
(450) 662-4942

Late June to late July
Lanaudière International Festival
Classical Music
(450) 759-7636

Late June to mid-July
Montréal International Jazz
Festival
(514) 871-1881

Late June
Strawberry picking season

JULY
July 1
Canada Day festivities
Downtown Montréal and Old
Port, Old Montréal
(514) 496-7678
Centennial Park
(514) 485-6806
Fort Lennox
(450) 291-5700
Montréal West
(514) 484-6186

To late July
Lanaudière International Festival
Classical Music
(450) 759-7636

Early July
Carifiesta
Downtown · Place-des-Arts Metro
(514) 735-2232

Early July
Powwow at Odanak Indian Village
(450) 568-2600

To mid-July
Montréal International Jazz
Festival
(514) 871-1881

Sundays
Benson & Hedges International
fireworks competition
La Ronde · Île Ste-Hélène metro
(514) 872-4537

Mid-late July
Just for Laughs
Family activities during day
Old Port
(514) 845-3155

Late July
Dragon Boat Race Festival
Olympic Basin
(514) 866-7001, 861-4816

Late July to early August
Les FrancoFolies de Montréal
French only – outdoor concerts,
many free
(514) 876-8989

AUGUST
Mid-August
Festival de Montgolfières (Hot
Air Balloons)
Saint Jean Sur Richelieu
(450) 346-6000

Mid-August
Sand Castle Competition
Parc Lafontaine
(514)522-2552

Harvest Festival
Cap St. Jacques Ecological Farm
(514) 280-6871

Fête de St. Louis
Fort Chambly
(450) 658-1585

Festival des Touts-Petits
Complexe Desjardins
(514) 524-5720

Late August
18th-century Public Market
Pointe-à-Callière
(514) 872-9132

SEPTEMBER
Labour Day Weekend
Brome Fair
(450) 242-3976

Mid-September
Powwow
Bonsecours Market
(514) 499-1854

Fall Colours
Ski resorts (Mt. Sutton,
Tremblant, etc.)

Apple picking season

OCTOBER
Oktoberfest
Morgan Arboretum
(514) 398-7811

Mid-Late October
Le Grand Bal des Citrouilles
(Grand Ball of the Pumpkins)
Botanical Garden
(514) 872-1400

Apple picking season

NOVEMBER
Early to mid-November
Coup de Coeur francophone
Celebration of French song
CEGEP Maisonneuve de la culture
Frontenac
Pie-IX or Frontenac Metro
(514) 872-2200

Early to mid-November
Santa Claus Parade
Downtown Montréal
(514) 252-9401

Mid-November
Salon du livre (Book Fair)
Place Bonaventure
Bonaventure Metro
(514) 397-2222

Mid-November
Montréal National Postage Stamp
Show
Place Bonaventure
Bonaventure Metro
(514) 397-2222

Mid-November to mid-February
Crèches display
St. Joseph's Oratory
(514) 733-8211

Mid-November to late December
The Christmas Village
Christmas display, choirs, Santa,
activities
Complexe Desjardins
(514) 845-4636

Late November
Montréal Model Train Show
Bonsecours Market

Late November
Montréal International Dog Show
Place Bonaventure
Bonaventure Metro
(514) 397-2222

Late November to early January
Christmas at the Museum
Montréal Museum of Fine Arts
Christmas concerts, activities for
families, 25 decorated trees
(514) 285-1600 · 1-800-515-0515

DECEMBER

To mid-February
Crèches display
St. Joseph's Oratory
(514) 733-8211

Early December
Noël des Chats
(Christmas Cat Show)
Place Bonaventure
(514) 397-2222

A Family Affair
McCord Museum holiday
activities
(514) 398-7100 ext. 234
www.mccord-museum.qc.ca

Christmas decorations
Place Montréal Trust
St. Catherine and McGill College
Peel or McGill Metro
(514) 843-8000

Ogilvy's Christmas Window
1307 St. Catherine West

Star of the Magi
Planetarium
(514) 872-4530

Christmas in the Garden
Botanical Garden
(514) 872-1400

Sundays in Advent
Living crèche
St. Joseph's Oratory, Pichette Hall
(514) 733-8211

The Nutcracker
Les grands Ballets canadiens
Salle Wilfrid-Pelletier,
Place des Arts
(514) 849-0269

INDEX

FREE OR ALMOST FREE

Notes

Notes

Notes

Notes

Notes

Notes

Notes

Notes

Notes

Notes